Psychic
Children

Psychic
Children

by Samuel H. Young

DOUBLEDAY & COMPANY, INC.
GARDEN CITY, NEW YORK, 1977

To Sally
for advice, patience,
and encouragement

ISBN: 0-385-07958-3
Library of Congress Catalog Card Number 76–24216

Contents

Preface

Nearly ten years ago a New York doctor told me of a curious encounter that proved to be the genesis of this book. Several weeks before, he said, a couple sought his advice about their eight-year-old daughter. It seemed the girl was seeing colors around people, a kind of fluid, multihued field which the child felt to be related in some way to people's moods. For example, the girl and some schoolmates had been acting up in class one day while the teacher's back was turned. Suddenly she noticed around the teacher's head a buildup of red, in a shade the child associated with anger. Quickly she went back to her work—just in time, it turned out. The teacher whirled about, catching the others in the act.

People's "colors" sometimes showed her more than their moods, the girl told her parents. The people she liked had "pretty" and "bright" colors around them, at least by comparison to what she saw around those few persons she disliked or mistrusted.

The doctor, who shared my interest in ESP, or, more properly, psi,* told the parents that seeing such colors, or "auras," was rare but by no means unheard of. They needn't think anything was wrong with the child, he said; in fact, it indicated a well-developed intuition which could prove very useful to her. He suggested they keep an open mind about the matter, listen attentively when the girl wanted to talk about her perceptions, but not make an issue of it. Perhaps the best approach, he said, would be to treat the ability as a modest asset, such as good co-ordination or an aptitude for a particular school subject—in short, as something that should be allowed to gradually integrate into her personality but not be stamped upon it.

The doctor's story stuck in my mind, accompanied by thoughts of the parents' extreme good fortune in being able to consult a doctor who was conversant in psi phenomena and who took a reasonable and rational approach to the subject. What were the odds that another family in a similar situation would receive such competent advice? What had happened in such instances in the past? Above all, what could be done to make available some necessary information and guidance concerning psychic perception in children?

Thus the idea for *Psychic Children* was born. It was nurtured over the next few years by my extensive research into the experiences of people who had been psychic as children, by consultations with leading parapsychologists, and by meeting some of the remarkable children I will presently discuss. As the research progressed, my own involvement in the subject grew from a journalist's avocation to a full-time position with a research association deeply involved in the study of psi. What also grew was my conviction that psi is by no means confined to a few exceptional children, but permeates every child's experience.

* I use the term "psi" to denote all types of psychic phenomena, of which extrasensory perception (ESP) and psychokinesis (PK) are principal components.

I have attempted to structure the book to alternate over-all views of how particular aspects of psi manifest in children's lives with informal profiles which illustrate how such psi has appeared in the childhood of several exceptional individuals. Thus the chapter on telepathy and clairvoyance is followed by the story of Jenny, whose life has constituted almost a continuing series of ESP events. Chapter Three, on psychokinesis, is followed by the account of Monica Lopez, whose remarkable healing abilities represent the use of PK to an almost miraculous degree. And so forth, through precognition and past-life memories to an exploration of fascinating "other worlds" encountered in countless childhoods.

Some anecdotes will inevitably challenge the credulity of many readers, as they did mine. Though I have not knowingly altered the facts (other than names) in any of the accounts which follow, and though I have been careful to quote only from sources I consider reliable, readers are encouraged to exercise their discernment. They are also asked to be tolerant of the religious milieus in which some of the events took place. Psi, I discovered, respects no cultural or conceptual boundaries. To follow it in its many guises requires a spontaneity that is impossible to maintain in the presence of narrow, sectarian attitudes.

The question may linger in some minds, why a book exclusively about the psychic experiences of children? Very simply, I feel that their need is the greatest. They stand to suffer the most damage from those who do not comprehend their particular sensitivity. They can also make the greatest gains through understanding and the proper encouragement. During my research one girl told me that she had learned to, in effect, turn her ESP on and off at will so that she was not too psychically vulnerable to disruptive personalities and situations. But as a child she was buffeted uncontrollably by these things. "It's hard for most people to understand," she said. "It was certainly hard for *me* to understand. But if only someone else nearby had known about it and I could have talked to them just once in a while, it would have been so different." Perhaps for many children in similar situations, *Psychic Children* will make such a difference.

I am indebted to many people for their help on this book. In addition to those mentioned in the text, there are numerous others whose replies to my questionnaires were invaluable. Special thanks for generous and timely assistance are owed to Laura Dale of the American Society for Psychical Research, Grazina Babusis of the Parapsychology Foundation, Isabelle Gaspar of the A.R.E. Library, and my colleagues in the Association for the Understanding of Man.

CHAPTER ONE

ESP: The Common Denominator

One afternoon, a Bloomington, Indiana, woman named Carolyn Mattingly was talking with her sister while the latter's two children played in the next room. The sister was expecting her third child and, perhaps inevitably, the conversation turned to selecting a name for the baby. As they talked, Carolyn remembered a list of names she had prepared several years before. She was about to mention the list, then stopped herself when she realized she had no idea where she had put it.

At that moment, her nephew stopped his playing and, without saying a word, went to a drawer in the kitchen, removed a piece of paper, and took it to his aunt. It was the list of names. Then, as if he had performed nothing more than some routine chore, the boy went back to his play.

The files of psychical research are filled with such cases. The only unusual element in this event is the likely presence, simultaneously, of both components of extrasensory perception (ESP): telepathy (communication between two or more beings by means independent of the normal senses) and clairvoyance (the extrasensory but nontelepathic perception of facts, objects, or events). The nephew evidently "picked up" telepathically his aunt's thoughts about the list of names. But since Carolyn Mattingly had no conscious knowledge of where she had put the list, it is apparent that, at the same moment, the nephew employed clairvoyance to find it.

Telepathy is perhaps the most elementary form of psychic perception, one which, researchers are coming to believe, every human experiences to some degree. Some parapsychologists go so far as to call it the commonest type of communication and assert that it operates more consistently than either words or actions produced in the conscious state. At the very least, it is the most common type of psi reported in relationship to children, due primarily to the frequent involvements of adults as agents (senders) or percipients (receivers) in telepathic incidents with children.

This was reflected in replies to a questionnaire I sent to leading parapsychologists. When I asked them to relate cases of psi in children, a significant number of them recounted episodes of telepathy in their own families. For example, Dr. Charles Tart of the University of California at Davis told me that "When my daughter, Cindy, was about five, she exhibited about a dozen clear-cut instances of telepathy from her mother. Every incident would take place with this type of pattern: my wife, Judy, would be doing some household task that didn't take too much attention and so left her mind free to wander, such as ironing or doing the dishes. She would be thinking about something totally unrelated to the task, and my daughter would wander into the room and make some comment about that subject or ask some question about the subject. These events happened over a period of several months and then just disappeared."

Dr. Berthold Schwarz, a New Jersey psychiatrist, has documented more then 1,500 cases of apparent telepathy in his own family, some 500 of which are recounted in his book *Parent-Child Telepathy.* "What happened between the children and their parents," Dr. Schwarz says of these cases, "was similar to, but simpler than, what happens frequently, at varying levels of consciousness, in (and out of!) the formal physician-patient psychotherapeutic sessions and to what might reasonably be surmised to happen on a far wider horizon between people of all ages." In almost every instance he recorded, Schwarz and his wife, Ardis, functioned as the agents and their children, Lisa and Eric, as percipients.

On one occasion, Ardis was having difficulty finding a baby-sitter. The regular sitter was unavailable and, because it was Christmas time, substitutes were scarce. Suddenly she remembered a woman who had been recommended to her many months ago, a Mrs. Axwell. At that moment, Lisa chimed in, "Mrs. Axwell, Mrs. Axwell." The child had never met the sitter and it was doubtful that she had ever heard her name.

In the kitchen one Sunday, Dr. Schwarz was reading a portion of a tomato juice can label that advertised initialed drinking glasses. Lisa, then two and a half, was sitting in a high chair at some distance from him and was not in a position to see the can. Suddenly she said, "New glasses, new glasses."

Again in the kitchen, on Lisa's first day of school, she was sitting at the table while breakfast was being prepared. Her father, nearby, spotted a collection of magazines on the counter and had to suppress his wish to pick up *Modern Medicine* and read it, since to do so at mealtime would have been impolite. Just then, Lisa got out of her chair, picked *Modern Medicine* out of the

3

pile, and handed it to her father. "She has never done this before and she cannot read," Dr. Schwarz noted.

Telepathy has also been in evidence in my own family. One morning when my son, John, was twenty-one months old, his mother lifted him from bed and was holding him up to a bedroom window so he could look outside. Sally wondered what she might point to and name that John would recognize, but there was not much to see besides trees and shrubbery. "Bush" crossed Sally's mind as she looked at the object nearest the window, but she was quite sure he had not heard the word, or at least did not know its meaning. Just then John pointed outside and said quite distinctly, "bush."

Several years later, we were driving home from a camping trip, when Sally began to reflect on the fact that John was due back in preschool the next day. Before our vacation, John had been afraid of thunderstorms, particularly if they occurred while he was at school. Sally wondered if this fear would still be with him. Just then, with no sensory cue from either of us—in fact, there had been no talk on any subject for many minutes—John brought up the subject of school and thunderstorms.

There is a rhyming game we sometimes play while traveling which is often good for a few "hits." One of us will choose a word, then we take turns naming words which rhyme with it (a popular entertainment for five-year-olds and a tolerable diversion for parents). On many occasions Sally will think of a word to find rhymes for, but before she can say it aloud, John will name the same word.

All these incidents, from Tart and Schwarz and from my family's experiences, seem to me to be typical of the kind of "routine" telepathic events one encounters in normal family situations. To my knowledge, none of those involved consider themselves especially psychic. The only irregular factor may be the ability of one or more of the family members to recognize these modest ESP events when they occur.

Equally routine, though more difficult to record, are incidents of telepathic communication between infants and their mothers. Many mothers are aware of a certain intuitive link with their babies which makes them sensitive to the child's needs, often without any overt cue from the child. A dramatic case of this involved a mother who dreamed one night that she was standing beside her baby's newly made grave. She awoke from the dream in a fright and rushed to the baby's bed, where she found him very pale, his breath coming fast and heavy. It took her some time to wake him, and by the time the doctor arrived the baby had gone into violent convulsions. The child survived, but only because of the mother's timely dream and quick response to it.

Some mothers have noticed that their babies are "tuned in" to them at certain embarrassing or inconvenient times. This happened to a physician's wife who became all too aware that, no matter where the baby was in the house or what he was doing, he would cry whenever his mother became sexually aroused. No doubt less troublesome was a pattern that emerged briefly in my son's infancy: whenever Sally sat down to eat, John would begin to cry—no matter if he were several rooms away. It occurred to us to keep a record of this, but the matter became such a nuisance that science bowed to convenience and John was usually brought to the table before the meal began. This effectively stopped the disruptions.

Similar to the anecdote of the mother whose dream warned her of her son in danger is a Cedarburg, Wisconsin, incident, reported by Dr. Ian Stevenson, in which Mrs. Oscar Hurth became dramatically aware that her five-year-old daughter, Joicey, was involved in an accident. Joicey had set out to join her father and brother at a movie theater a block and a half from home. Her mother was drying the dinner dishes, quite confident that

5

the child could safely make the short journey by herself. Suddenly Mrs. Hurth experienced what she described as an "awesome feeling" which caused her to drop the plate she was drying. "Oh, God, don't let her get killed!" she prayed. She had just received a strong impression that Joicey had been or was about to be hit by a car.

Mrs. Hurth rushed to the phone and dialed the theater. "My little girl was on the way to the theater," she told the woman who answered. "She has had an accident. Is she badly hurt?" The woman at the theater seemed stunned. "How did you know?" The accident had just happened, she said. The woman asked Mrs. Hurth to hold the phone. While she waited, the mother could hear the ambulance siren. By now she was almost frantic.

Then the theater manager came on the phone. In a calm voice he explained that Joicey had been struck by a car but was not seriously hurt. Her father was with her and she was receiving a doctor's care. In fact, she was well enough to go to the movie; only a swollen lip, some facial bruises, and a soiled dress remained as evidence of the accident.

Laura Dale of the American Society for Psychical Research has reported a similar case, though this time both parent and child seem to have acted as agents and percipients. A six-year-old boy had gone to a beach on Long Island Sound with his sisters. While there, the boy got into a tiny, very tippy boat and, before anyone could stop him, he was carried out toward the sea. At that moment, the mother, who was at the home some six miles away, had a strong feeling that this was happening. In fact, she seemed to hear her son calling, "Mommy! Mommy!" Feeling helpless, as she had no car to drive to the beach, the mother fell to her knees and prayed that the boy would be helped, that he would remain seated in the boat and not stand up. She seemed to know, she said later, that if he stood up he would be lost.

Anxious hours later, she learned that the boy had been rescued. He had been saved, the rescuers said, because he had not stood and tipped the boat.

Of course, telepathy is not limited to parent and child. Many instances of telepathy between siblings have also been documented. Dr. Louisa Rhine has recounted an incident which occurred when two young brothers briefly separated. One was taken to visit his grandmother, a block and a half from his home, where he would spend the night, while the other stayed at home. In less than an hour, the boy who stayed at home ran to his mother sobbing, "Chris wants you, Mommy." The mother insisted that he must be mistaken. It was then 2:10 P.M. Presently, the grandmother arrived at the door with Chris, who was in tears. He had awakened from his nap, she said, crying for his mother. The time he awoke, she said, had been 2:10.

A fascinating aspect of children's telepathy is that experienced between twins. A study of both identical and fraternal twins conducted in Canada indicated that telepathic incidents between twins were far more frequent than between one twin and other individuals. "Her decisions are so similar to my own," said one girl of her twin. "Questions asked by my twin are often identical to those asked by me." "We both think the same things at the same time and I can tell what her feelings are," said another. Other comments made to the Canadian researchers were similar: "I always know her mood without talking to her or even seeing her"; "We both say the same thing at once. In the store, if I don't feel like waiting on a customer and I want my brother to, he usually does"; "This afternoon, when I was going to ask her for some money, she asked me if I wanted some. She seemed to know." One boy reported that his intuitive rapport with his twin brother was particularly useful in sports, especially basketball and hockey. "I never have to look to know where he is," he said. "I just shoot the puck."

In a separate study, Professor H. H. Newman of the University of Chicago observed a pair of girls who seemed able to telepathically communicate answers to one another during school exams. In one instance, they had been pressed for time while studying for the exam, so each twin reviewed half the course material. Their test answers were so similar that they might have been accused of cheating had they not taken the precaution of sitting far apart in the examination room.

Outside the family, school sometimes provides another environment conducive to ESP. A number of formal ESP tests given in schools have indicated the presence of both telepathy and clairvoyance in classroom situations. Students tended to demonstrate the highest degree of ESP when the test was administered by a familiar home-room teacher rather than by a stranger, or by a teacher well liked by students rather than one less popular. In fact, research parapsychologist Dr. Rex Stanford has ventured the opinion that a warm, fluid relationship between teacher and students might favor ESP to the extent that material peripheral to that actually being discussed is picked up telepathically by the students. In other words, Dr. Stanford suggests, a teacher well versed in a subject and in rapport with the students may unconsciously convey to the class some information which helps foster an understanding of that being verbally expounded.

Dr. Stanford is no stranger to ESP in the classroom. Though he does not claim to be particularly psychic himself, he was aware of ESP from an early age and sought to use it to his advantage at school. Before exams, he would get permission to keep relevant school books in a closed briefcase next to him. His idea was that he might be able to, if necessary, "tune in" clairvoyantly on the appropriate material. He is not prepared to say whether this practice helped him at all, but colleagues report that he was a straight-A student throughout school and college.

Recent research indicates that the young Rex Stanford might

have been onto something. A Swedish parapsychologist working in Holland supervised a number of tests in which students were given, in addition to a sheet of test questions, an opaque envelope in which answers to some of the questions had been written out. The students could not open the envelopes and could not read the answers through the opaque covering, yet they scored significantly better on those questions that had been answered. Evidently they had some extrasensory awareness of what was inside the envelopes.

What seems to me to be a striking case of clairvoyance was demonstrated to me by a girl in Port Arthur, Texas. When I spoke with her, Angela (not her real name) was in her early teens and lived with her parents in a modest white frame house. She was an honor student at school, gave piano lessons, and, since age eight, had played the organ at church.

If she were told a person's age, name, and the town where they lived, Angela said, she was sometimes able to get accurate impressions about them. As an example, she told me of a case involving an eighteen-year-old girl. "At first when I tried to tune in on her, I saw a real pretty girl, smiling and happy. But then, a few seconds later, I saw another girl, with a scary face, real mean-looking. She didn't last long, either. Then the first girl appeared again and the same thing happened all over. I tried to hold onto one image long enough to find out something, but it was hard. Finally I was able to picture both girls, and the two of them came together and formed one person. But I could tell there was a big clash between them.

"I didn't know what this was all about, so my father got in touch with the people who had given us the girl's name. They said my impression was pretty accurate because the girl was schizophrenic and in an institution.

"Another time," Angela continued, "an uncle of mine who lives in Central America was visiting here and asked me to locate

9

a dog of his he'd lost back home. I said I would and went to my room and relaxed. All of a sudden, like a picture being drawn in my mind, I saw a dog. And then a house started appearing with a white picket fence around it. After that, two intersecting streets showed up and a street light and then some buildings in the background. The dog came down one of the streets, went past the house with the picket fence, and continued on around the corner. But I couldn't follow him any farther than that.

"All during this I was looking for a street sign, and finally I saw one. But it didn't have anything on it. It was just plain white. So I waited and asked to see some letters on the sign. An 'A' began to form and then a 'P' right before it, and then a 'T.' After that came a few blurry letters I couldn't make out. So what I had was 'Pat.'

"Then the dog went into the house with the picket fence and didn't come out. I tried to get into the house or around the street corner, but I couldn't. That was all the information I could get, I figured, so I got up and came back in the living room here and told my uncle what I saw.

"My impressions made most sense to my uncle's daughter, who was here, too. She said she had a sister-in-law back home named Patricia and that Patricia had always wanted the dog. She was always asking to take care of it, but they'd refused. Then one day after some kind of argument with Patricia, they couldn't find the dog. Their friends told them Patricia had the dog, but when they went to her house (it was on a street corner and had a white picket fence, just like I'd seen it) they couldn't find it. Later, other friends said they'd seen Patricia with the dog, but my uncle and his daughter could never catch her with it.

"They were real surprised at what I told them because they knew I'd never heard of Patricia or known anything about her home. I never did find out if they got the dog back."

At this point in the interview, Angela was asked if she would be willing to demonstrate her ability. She quickly agreed. After being told the name and age of a man in a city some two hundred miles to the west, Angela settled into her chair. Almost at once, she began to relate her impressions.

"Well, the first thing I see is something like a yellowish light about an inch and a half across the head area. I really don't know what it is, but it could be hair. In the neck area I see that the muscles are real, real tight. I see a lot of tension, like he's been overexercising.

"As I go down, it seems like the muscles are real sore in the shoulders, though more so on the right. I see the heart pumping fast, but I'm not sure if this is happening now or is a little in the past or future."

She paused. "Does he limp? I see a sort of limp when he walks." There was another short pause. "All of a sudden, it seems like he's in great pain. He's grabbing his left side and is kind of bent over. He's breathing real heavy, but I can't pinpoint where the pain is." As she said this, Angela put her right hand to her left side, at the base of the rib cage.

Now there was a longer pause. Then, "He looks like he has a great amount of energy to put out, and he seems like he's psychic. Energy patterns seem to come to him and he breaks them down into a form. This has a lot to do with his eyes, as if sparks of energy come to him and he uses them to make forms.

"There is a woman beside him. She is about five feet seven and has her hair done up like this, and then it comes down like this in big curls." Angela outlined the shape of a hairdo with her hands. "The hair seems black. I see her standing on his right side and a little behind him." Angela indicated that she had no further impressions of the subject. She showed no curiosity as to whether or not she was correct, but waited quietly for additional questions.

11

Actually, it would have been difficult at that moment to verify much of what she had said. The person in question was a friend of mine who had been in a minor car accident several days before. I knew that the accident had left him stiff and sore, but I had no idea of the specific areas of pain. I could also verify that he walked with a limp and that his wife was approximately the height described, though Angela's description of her light brown hair as black seemed a definite miss. Thus, though perhaps half of the information Angela gave me could have been gleaned from me telepathically, the other half was definitely outside my conscious awareness.

My friend later confirmed that Angela's description of his pain was completely accurate. She had even described precisely his position in the car immediately after the accident. The "sparks" of energy she had talked of were very descriptive, he said, of a recent dream in which he saw himself with hundreds of light points dancing before his eyes. And Angela's impression of the wife's hairdo seemed uncanny. The latter had had her hair arranged that day in a completely new style—in the very manner Angela indicated.

It is not often that one encounters an Angela, who can produce on cue such a degree of attunement with distant subjects. More often, clairvoyance manifests among children in spontaneous situations around the home. An eminent parapsychologist wrote me that "When my youngest was old enough to play simple card games with me, she often 'knew' what a concealed card would be. I don't remember age exactly, but perhaps the range of ages was four to ten. She was a gentle, cooperative, darling youngster and always restructured games with me so that the loser would have enough chances to win, too; every game had to end as a draw. She was cooperating with me in having mild pleasure, not fully competing with me, in these games."

Others have reported cases of children able to locate lost or deliberately concealed objects. Robert E. L. Masters told me of an eight-year-old girl he had met, the daughter of a well-known film director, who, once shown an object, could then find it weeks or even months later, wherever it might be in her house, just by closing her eyes and receiving an image of its whereabouts.

Children also have demonstrated an aspect of clairvoyance called psychometry, which is the ability to provide verifiable information about an object by extrasensory means. In a test conducted by Dr. Charles Thomas Cayce, an eleven-year-old girl was given thirteen different objects she had never seen before and was asked to describe their owners and provide whatever additional data she could. Six of the objects were so accurately described as to be scored "hits," while four were partial hits, and three scored as misses.

A teen-ager I will call Linda told me that when she was in first or second grade she was taken with her school class to a museum, where she received a number of impressions about a re-created sixteenth-century French room. Quite spontaneously, she began to describe various objects in the room, explaining what they were, how they were made, who made them, etc. She stopped only when she noticed the shocked expressions on the faces of her teacher and the museum guide. Fortunately for Linda, her parents were aware of her psychometric ability—in fact, her mother learned to value Linda's intuitions about the authenticity of antiques and always took her along when shopping for them—and were able to give the school some palliative explanation.

During a conversation with Linda, I handed her a metal cross approximately five inches high and asked her what impressions she received from it. After a few moments she said, "I get the feeling of a dome," then, after another pause, "I also feel heat. But that's all." Until recently the cross had been mounted on the

13

top of a domed church lantern. Candles had been burned in the lantern directly under the dome, which obviously made the cross quite hot.

My conversation with Linda involved still another aspect of clairvoyance. "For as long as I can remember," she said, "I've been able to see auras. I remember seeing all kinds of things around people when I was little and not knowing what they meant because I hadn't studied what the colors and formations meant. Now, it is a tremendous part of my life—in meeting people, just 'checking them out,' and in some cases helping them.

"I see the aura around the entire person," Linda continued. "It's like an enveloping egg, with layers of colors, different levels of energy, which I interpret as belonging to three different categories: physical, mental-emotional, and spiritual. It is all color and light interacting, constantly moving as your thoughts and bodily conditions change. The spiritual area, which I see farther out, doesn't change as much. It is more established, if the person has developed it at all. The aura is really the energy sent off from the person at all levels of being, showing the condition of the person at the time. One example is when a person tells a lie. I see a slash go through the aura, or particles go shooting out. The color in these cases is acid green, an ugly yellow-green.

"In many people," Linda said, "there are sometimes little patterns, like doodles, of very concentrated-type energy. Some people call them thought forms. With you," she said while looking disconcertingly above my head, "maybe because of what you're doing now, I can see them inside your aura working out. Mostly round shapes that are very three-dimensional and several shades of blue. They seem to relate to your purpose in asking me these questions, as if they're telling me it's O.K."

When I pressed for a further description of my aura, however, Linda became reluctant. A certain amount of fatigue was evident, she said, which looked "sort of like wet feathers" and a

14

head cold I was then suffering manifested as "a murky kind of brownish green" around the bridge of my nose and my lower forehead. There was also a lot of yellow, denoting mental activity, around my head, she said, and the yellow bulged out a bit on the right. But that is all she was inclined to say. I considered none of this particularly evidential at the time. However, subsequent interviews with other children who also claimed to see auras, though generally inconclusive as well, produced two more observations about yellow around my head which bulged significantly to the right. None of the subjects were able to explain that particular configuration. Nor am I. But it does indicate that something more than imagination was involved.

One of these later encounters was with an engaging young New Yorker I will call Jenny. Her ESP appeared so extensive and so evidential that, at minimum, a chapter is needed to tell her story.

CHAPTER TWO

Jenny

"It's going to be awful! My party is going to be ruined! Call if off, Mommy, *please* call it off!"

Mira Kasten, half awake, struggled to understand what her daughter was saying. In the dim morning light she could barely see the tears on Jenny's face, the look of near-panic in the child's eyes as she sobbed forlornly by the bed.

"Darling, everything is going to be all right. You just had a bad dream. Isn't that right?"

"But it was so real. It was my party. Susan and Jean came. We didn't invite them but they came anyway and ruined everything. They pulled off the tablecloth and wouldn't play any of the party games. Finally you called their mothers and told them to come take them home. But do you know what? Their mothers wouldn't come, so you had to send them home with the housekeeper." Jenny paused, remembering. Then she wailed, "They

17

were so mean they even took back the presents they brought me!"

"Listen," Mira said, "Susan and Jean aren't invited to your party. If they do try to come, we just won't let them in. It's as simple as that. So what's there to worry about?"

"I guess you're right."

"Of course I'm right."

Jenny located some tissues on Mira's bedside table, dabbed at her eyes, and blew her nose. Then she was still for a moment, recalling something more.

"Wait a minute!" Her face brightened. "That couldn't have been *my* party. The decorations were different. We bought Mexican decorations, didn't we?"

"That's right."

"Well, in the dream there were Charlie Brown decorations. You know, pictures of Linus and Snoopy and all. They were on the tablecloth and the napkins and hats. So it couldn't have been my party. Yes, and I remember now: It must have been someone else's house! There was a living room with a light green rug and sofas with a beautiful green print on them. It looked like trees in a forest. And in the dining room was a big, big cabinet like the one we used to have."

"Like the armoire?"

"Yes! Oh, I feel so much better. It all seemed like it was really happening. I just wonder whose place it was?"

"It was a *dream* place, Jenny. You probably made it up."

"Well, it seemed more real than that."

The child stood by the bed several moments more, then shrugged, turned, and walked briskly out of her mother's bedroom.

Mira watched her go, marveling at how quickly Jenny could go from near-hysterics to complete calm. She was usually a serene, self-possessed child, easily the best-adjusted individual in

18

the family. But there seemed to be some mechanism inside her that could produce such sudden emotions as the near-panic Mira had just witnessed. This did not happen often, but Mira had learned to recognize and respect this strange sensitivity. Though disguised in irrational, emotional behavior, more than once it had proven to be communicating something quite real to the child, something neither Jenny nor anyone else around her could have perceived through the so-called normal senses. As her daughter disappeared into the gloom of the hallway, Mira wondered what this morning's episode might mean.

Mira had her answer two months later. Jenny's eighth birthday party came and went without mishap. Then came an invitation to a party for a girl in Jenny's class at school. Jenny was not sure she wanted to go. The girl was not a close friend, at least not so close that either had visited the other's home. But the whole class had been invited. It might appear rude, she decided, if she did not attend.

Mira drove Jenny to the girl's apartment building and saw that she got safely onto the elevator. "Remember, call me when it's over and I'll pick you up."

"I will."

The call came sooner than expected. "Mommy, can you come get me?" Mira thought she heard a note of panic in Jenny's voice.

"Of course."

"When you get here, come upstairs. *Please* come upstairs."

"Why, sure."

Mira was met at the door by a woman who looked harried and abstracted, as if she were keeping a tight but uncertain grip on herself. She showed Mira into the living room, then went to find Jenny.

Mira looked around. The light green carpet and the sofas

covered in a handsome green print gave her the feeling that she had been there before.

Jenny appeared at that moment, took Mira by the hand, and led her to the dining room. There, on the table and scattered around the floor, were the crumpled, soiled remains of the party decorations: a paper tablecloth, napkins and party hats, all covered with "Peanuts" characters. Against the far wall was a large armoire similar to the one Mira once owned.

"This is it, Mommy! This is the party I dreamed about. Susan and Jean came and caused a lot of trouble. They pulled off the tablecloth, spilling everything, and wouldn't play any of the games. It was terrible. So the mother called their homes and asked *their* mothers to come take them home. But they refused to come, so the housekeeper here had to take them home. *And they took back their presents!*"

The harried mother reappeared. Mira learned from her that everything had happened at the party just as Jenny described it. And as Jenny had dreamed it two months before.

It was another item for Mira's journal, a precognitive dream that was accurate except for Jenny's initial misidentification of the schoolmate's birthday party with her own.

Mira began the journal when Jenny was four. In it she recorded all the curious incidents in Jenny's life—sometimes two and three per week, other times no more than one a month—which, considered together, indicate the child has pronounced ESP.

Jenny is now fourteen, an engaging girl with dark eyes, dark hair, and a voice surprisingly resonant for someone so small and slender. Her home is a large, comfortable Manhattan apartment filled with active people. Harold Kasten, Jenny's stepfather, is a financial analyst who reports each day to an office on Wall Street. He is a tall man in his forties who seems at once both

20

tense and easygoing. Mira, bright, informal, talkative, has a controlling interest in a family business and is the driving force behind a foundation which promotes and supports psychical research. Jenny's sixteen-year-old brother, Mark, is a straight-A student with straight black hair he wears down to his shoulders. He is an accomplished photographer and budding parapsychologist. Jenny herself is a good athlete and gets straight A's in school, though she is said to be the most effortless achiever in the family.

The focal point of the household is a compact library where, on a typical afternoon, the telephone seems to ring incessantly. Callers may include a parapsychologist who wants to know how Mira is progressing with the fund-raising for his dream research, or a representative of a TV talk show who has heard that Mira is a close friend of the young Israeli psychic Uri Geller. Could she persuade Uri to make an appearance? Or, just as likely, it is a friend of Mark or Jenny, soliciting advice, trading gossip, making plans.

Between calls, Mira Kasten jokes that it is Jenny who is to blame for all the commotion in their home. She was the one who made Mira aware there *is* such a thing as ESP and who got her hooked on the subject.

It began almost as soon as Jenny could talk, Mira explains. Mira was then married to Jenny's father and they lived in a suburb of New York. At first, there were little incidents which seemed to indicate that Jenny was picking up Mira's thoughts. Mira dismissed these as coincidences until they occurred so often she began to pay closer attention.

There was the time, for example, when three-year-old Jenny was standing in her crib while her mother selected a dress for her from a closet around a corner, out of Jenny's sight. Mira picked out a red dress. Just then Jenny said, "Mommy, I wore that one yesterday."

21

"What one?"

"The red one."

It was Jenny's only red dress. Mira remembered that the child had, in fact, worn it the day before. But how could Jenny know it was the red one she now held in her hand? There was no way the child could have spotted it from her crib—no mirrors, no reflections in the windowpanes, and no direct line of sight.

On another occasion, Mira had developed a splitting headache but was too involved in housework to stop and get herself an aspirin. Jenny, who had been playing quietly in her room, suddenly appeared in the kitchen with a bottle of children's aspirin she had taken from the bathroom. Coupled with Mira's shock that the child had gotten into the medicine cabinet was her amazed discovery that Jenny had sensed her discomfort telepathically.

And there was the time Jenny's father lost his pearl tie pin. It had been an anniversary present to him from Mira, which made its loss especially upsetting. As he and Mira were searching around their bedroom, Jenny wandered in and asked what they were doing.

"Daddy has lost his tie pin," Mira explained. "Have you seen it?" Jenny looked puzzled. "Do you know what I'm talking about?"

"No."

"It's a long, straight pin with a pearl on the end of it. He wears it all the time with his tie. You mean you've never noticed it?"

"Oh, that." Jenny looked at her father seriously. "Don't worry, Daddy, I'll find it."

Jenny's parents exchanged smiles as the child frowned in concentration like some tiny conjuror. Moments later she walked from the bedroom saying, "Follow me."

She led them out the front door and down the driveway to a pile of leaves. Jenny reached into the pile.

"Here it is!" She held up a pearl that was precisely the size of the one on the tie pin. But there was no pin. Evidently, the pearl had become detached from the pin and fell into the leaf pile while Jenny's father had been getting in or out of his car.

Though grateful for the recovery of the pearl, Jenny's father was unmoved by this evidence of his daughter's ESP. He was a successful New York lawyer. Reality to him was what could be proven scientifically or established "beyond a reasonable doubt" in a court of law. Reality was definitely *not* his own daughter clairvoyantly "tuning in" on a lost object. He resented these little episodes and became so annoyed when Mira began to keep a record of them that he insisted she stop.

This was only one of the strains between Jenny's parents, one symptom of a marital split that gradually, irrevocably widened. Though the couple had taken pains to conceal their difficulties from friends, parents, and especially their two children, Jenny somehow knew what was happening. Often while her husband slept, Mira lay awake at night, crying softly. From her room, far down the hall and well out of earshot, Jenny would call out to her. When Mira went to her, the child would say sleepily, "Poor Mommy. Mommy's crying. Mommy's so sad."

The break came when Jenny was seven. Mira and the two children went to live with Mira's parents in Brooklyn. It was a large, loving and fun-filled household. Not only were there grandparents to adore Jenny, but "Nana," Jenny's great-grandmother, lived there as well. In this atmosphere, Jenny's ESP seemed to increase. Mira, free from her husband's disapproval, once again made entries in her journal and began to read books about ESP.

A favorite game in the new home was Scrabble. All the

23

women played it, including Jenny, who had her own "Junior Scrabble" set. Jenny always won.

It didn't make sense. The girl was only seven. Her vocabulary was much smaller than the others'. Yet she beat even Mira's mother, who had developed an enormous vocabulary during years of doing crossword puzzles.

"How come you always let me win?" Jenny protested one day. "Is it because I'm a little girl? Why don't any of you really play?"

"We *are* playing," Mira insisted. "You always win because you draw the high-scoring letters. You always get the exact ones you need to make a seven-letter word or get a triple word score. You're lucky and we're not."

"Well, why don't *you* draw the letters you want?"

"How can we?" Mira held up the brown felt bag from which the players drew their letters.

"*I* can do it."

The women looked at one another. Perhaps she *could* select the letters she needed. When you came down to it, that seemed the most logical explanation for the fact that Jenny could then— and can now—beat anyone at Scrabble by one hundred fifty to two hundred points.

It was through a Scrabble game during a visit with her father that Jenny was able to overcome his skepticism about her ESP. Frustrated at being beaten by her, he demanded to know how she kept getting seven-letter words.

"It's simple," she said. "You can, too, if you want to learn how to draw them."

"What are you talking about? Listen, I have four letters in my hand now. If I drew the right three, I would have a seven-letter word."

"Which three?"

"M, B, and E."

Jenny remembers, "I was so scared. If I could make *him* believe, I could make *anybody* believe. So I closed my eyes and said a prayer and put my hand in the bag and pulled out the letters M, B, and E. He kind of screamed and then telephoned my mother."

"O.K.," he told Mira, "she's got ESP!"

Mira married Harold Kasten when Jenny was eight. Jenny continued to flourish. She made friends easily and got excellent grades in school. The same was true of Mark, with the difference, Mira noted, that the boy worked harder for his high scores. Yet he was much more intellectual, more "scholarly" in his approach to things, which contrasted with Jenny's seemingly effortless, even casual, attitude toward schoolwork. More than once Mira wondered if Jenny's ESP helped her anticipate what questions were going to be asked on a test, or perhaps enabled her to pick up answers that the teacher had in mind.

There was the time, for example, when no one in class, including Jenny, had read an assigned history lesson about the caste system in India. When the teacher asked a question about it, Jenny had a silly urge and volunteered to answer: "Well, the book talks about a carpenter from one caste who works for an important man in the village. The rich man is very nice to the carpenter, and even feeds him. But he wouldn't think of eating *with* him." Jenny was astonished when the teacher nodded and said how glad he was that at least one person in the class had read the assigned passage.

But neither Mira nor Jenny wanted to give these matters undue emphasis. At most, they saw them as evidence of an unusual talent which Jenny took for granted and which Mira, out of a mother's concern, sought to understand. Few outside of the immediate family knew about her ESP, which was the way both mother and daughter preferred it. The small, dark-eyed child was intelligent, poised, unusually considerate of others, and had a quiet, playful sense of humor. These things seemed more than sufficient for Jenny to make her way in the world. The ESP, perhaps, was just a bonus.

Still, it was a bonus that could come in handy. Jenny always seemed to know when and where Mira could find a parking space. She had uncanny luck finding money in the street, and could go to a row of pay telephones and determine, without first looking, which ones had change left in the coin return. And on some occasions she could send telepathic messages.

Once, for example, Jenny came home from school and found no one there. Mira, who had a job downtown, was almost always home by then. Jenny became worried and called her grandmother in Brooklyn.

"Don't worry, darling. She probably ran into traffic. I'm sure she'll be home soon. By the way, I want you to give her a message for me."

"O.K."

"Tell her I'm going out tomorrow night and I need those antique earrings she took to be repaired for me. You know the ones?"

"Yes."

"You'll tell her?"

"Yes, Grandma. What store did she take them to?"

"Janet Brown."

"O.K. I'll tell her."

At that moment, Mira was heading home in a taxi. She was reading a book, oblivious of her surroundings.

Suddenly, a strange shock passed through her body. She looked up, slammed the book to the seat, and practically shouted for the cabdriver to turn the taxi around and head back downtown—to Janet Brown, on Sixtieth between Madison and Fifth.

"This is crazy," Mira thought. "Why this sudden compulsion

to pick up Mother's earrings?" Her mother, knowing that Mira's office was near Janet Brown, had asked her to stop for them—*at her convenience*. Here she was, already late getting home, going back downtown on an errand she could easily do some other day.

The cab waited outside the shop while Mira dashed inside for the earrings. Then they headed uptown again.

The moment Mira walked into the apartment, Jenny called out, "Did you get my message?"

"What message?"

"About Janet Brown. Grandma's earrings."

"What on earth do you mean?"

"Grandma told me to ask you to pick up her earrings. So I sent you the message."

"How did you do it?"

"I just spoke the name of the store three times."

Mira checked with her mother to find out when she had phoned Jenny. The time was just moments before Mira had gotten the sudden urge in the taxi to turn back and pick up the earrings.

Not long after, Jenny's grandmother played a part in another ESP episode. The family was rushing through dinner one evening so that Mark and a tableful of his friends would be in time for a rock concert. Mira was going to drive them downtown. Halfway through the meal, just as Mira was glancing nervously at her watch, the phone rang. It was Aunt Addy, Grandma's sister.

Her husband was terribly sick, Addy said. But he refused to be taken to the hospital in an ambulance. She had called her sister, hoping that she and her husband could take them, but the nurse who cared for Nana, Jenny's great-grandmother, said the couple had gone out. Were they with Mira?

"No," Mira said. "They went out for dinner and then they're going to a movie."

27

"Well, if they should call in the next fifteen minutes, please tell them to call me."

"Of course, Addy." There was a pause, long enough for Mira to sense what her aunt expected of her. "I'll tell you what," Mira said. "If Mother calls within fifteen minutes, I'll give her the message. If not, Harold and I will come down and take you ourselves."

"Thank you, Mira."

That, Mira thought, was all she needed, the rush of getting Mark and his friends downtown, the drive to Brooklyn to take Uncle Arthur to the hospital—not to mention the red tape of getting him admitted—then the race back to Manhattan to pick up the kids after the concert.

Jenny, seeing the distress on Mira's face, asked what was the matter. Her mother quickly explained.

"Do you want me to send Grandma a message?"

At that moment Mira would have done almost anything to resolve her predicament. "Sure. Why not?"

"What do you want me to tell her?"

Mira thought. They would all be leaving shortly, so there would be no one here to give her the message. But Nana's nurse knew the situation. "Tell Grandma to call her home."

Jenny went to her room and stood in front of the full-length mirror. She felt odd, unsure of what she was going to do, not to mention how she was going to do it, but she was confident that it would work.

She looked at her image in the mirror, concentrating on it until she was conscious of nothing else. Suddenly, her reflection vanished. She knew it was the moment to send the message. "Grandma, call home. Grandma, call home. Grandma, call home." She waited. Then there was a "click" somewhere inside her head. At that moment she knew the message had been received.

Mira drove Mark and his friends to the concert. Then she called her mother's house. Her mother was there.

"What are *you* doing home?" Mira knew how she treasured her infrequent nights out, away from Nana's demands.

"Uncle Arthur is sick. We drove him to the hospital."

"I know he's sick. Addy called me trying to find out where you had gone. But how did *you* find out?"

"Mira, it's the strangest thing. You know I never call home once I go out. Nana would insist we come right back and then get upset if we didn't. God forbid I do that to you someday! But tonight I just *had* to call, don't ask me why."

"What time did you call?"

"It was seven twenty-five. I remember because when I went to the phone your father told me the time and said we'd be late for the show."

"Would you believe that at seven twenty-five Jenny tried to send you a message to call home?"

"Oh, no wonder!"

Perhaps it was inevitable that Jenny's ESP would become known outside her family. No matter how certain Mira was that it was genuine and a well-integrated part of her daughter's life, she knew that many people were apt to feel differently. The best way to protect Jenny, then, was to conceal the fact. But this did not always work.

One day Mira drove Mark to a movie in midtown. Jenny, then seven, was in the back seat of the car.

They were just leaving the garage when Jenny asked, "Mommy, if a man in a big truck, a man who can't speak English, bangs into our car and doesn't hurt us but smashes the car, do we have to pay to get the car fixed?"

"What an odd question! No, dear, the insurance company would pay."

29

"What's an insurance company?"

Mira explained. But Jenny seemed skeptical. "Are you sure we wouldn't have to pay?" she persisted.

"Yes, I'm quite sure."

Traffic grew heavier as they approached midtown. At the busy intersection of Third Avenue and Fifty-ninth Street, they stopped at a red light. An enormous dump truck to their left gunned its motor, then, anticipating the green light, began to inch steadily into their lane. Evidently, the driver intended to make a right turn from the left lane and was too high up to notice Mira's Mustang beside him. As in a nightmare in slow motion, the huge machine plowed into the car, pushing it up onto the sidewalk. At last, the driver realized what was happening and stopped.

But for Mira the nightmare continued. The Mustang was badly crumpled. She and the children seemed all right—there hadn't been a collision, just a slow, terrifying shove, so there was little chance of injury, but Jenny was crying hysterically. Pedestrians gawked. Several lawyers handed Mira their cards. Policemen asked Mira insinuating and confusing questions. And the driver of the truck shrugged helplessly when Mira addressed him; he spoke no English.

At last the Mustang was towed to a garage, Mark was delivered to his movie, and the police and spectators went their ways. But Jenny was still crying. Mira hailed a taxi and took her to a pediatrician. The pediatrician sent them on to a neurologist who could examine the child for a possible head injury.

But the neurologist found nothing wrong. "Jenny," he said, "you don't even need an X-ray. Do you really think you were hurt?"

"No."

"Then why are you crying?"

"Because it was my fault!" Jenny sobbed.

30

"What was your fault?"

"I knew the accident was going to happen and I didn't tell Mommy!" This confession seemed to lift a great burden from the child. Her crying subsided.

Now it was Mira who felt like crying. As if her earlier ordeals hadn't been enough, she would now have to find some plausible excuse for Jenny's remark. And the doctor looked difficult to fool. "Please, God, get us out of here," Mira thought.

The neurologist seemed to be pondering what Jenny had said. "What do you mean when you say you knew the accident was going to happen?"

"It's nothing," Mira interposed. "She had a little premonition, that's all."

"Would you describe it for me, the premonition?"

"Well, there's really not much to tell you. After what she's been through, I think I should get Jenny home."

The doctor smiled. "I understand your reluctance, but I have a real interest in this. I studied ESP for a while at Duke."

"Well, that makes a difference!" Happy to be able to talk freely about the day's events, Mira related the story in detail.

The doctor seemed impressed. Before they left, he gave Jenny a brief test for clairvoyance, using a special deck of colored cards. Mira waited in another room during the test to avoid any psychic interference her presence might cause. Presently, Jenny and the doctor emerged.

The doctor seemed excited. "It's only my first impression," he said, "but it certainly looks like you've got one."

"Got one what?" Mira laughed. "A child with ESP?"

"That's just what I mean. A child with ESP. Lots of it!"

Other ESP tests came later. In one conducted at Brooklyn's Maimonides Hospital, Jenny and three adults who were considered to have pronounced ESP were asked to describe a number

31

of art prints that had been carefully sealed inside two opaque envelopes. Jenny received the highest score, effectively describing fourteen of thirty-six cards that were completely concealed from her vision.

Mira tested her too. It seemed a game to Jenny as she tried to guess the sequence of printed symbols—stars, circles, wavy lines, squares, or crosses—in Mira's deck of Zener cards. She knew that five correct guesses in a "run" of twenty-five cards was an average, or "chance," score, so she tried to surpass this. At first Jenny scored seven, eight, and nine hits, significantly above chance. But, not satisfied, she kept working with the cards until she was averaging seventeen, eighteen, and nineteen hits per run.

Jenny also scored well when she was asked to guess the future sequence of cards in a deck that had not yet been shuffled, a common test for precognition. However, when she realized what she was doing, she refused to continue. "It's impossible! It can't be done!" she insisted, and that was that.

Jenny sometimes produced impressive test results even when she didn't want to. Because the card tests were like games to her, she looked forward with childish impatience to her sessions with Mira. So she was quite upset one evening when Mira told her that there wasn't time to run a test; Mira and Harold were expected at a dinner party and Mira needed the time to dress.

"But you *promised!*" Jenny complained.

"I'm sorry, dear, there just isn't time. We'll do all the tests you want tomorrow."

Jenny sulked. She could understand the situation, of course, but that did not make her feel better. So when Mira appeared in the hall, dressed for the party, Jenny shot off a remark she knew would annoy her.

"You're always telling us how important it is to keep our word, right?"

"Yes, I've said that."

"Well, just remember you broke a promise today."

Mira flushed. "All right. If you're going to have that attitude, we'll do the cards right now." She marched into the library and pulled the Zener deck from a drawer. "We'll be late, thanks to you, but if this is so terribly *important,* we'll just do a run now."

Jenny hadn't anticipated this reaction. To save face, she feigned indifference to the cards. In fact she deliberately called out wrong answers.

It worked. Every answer was wrong. "That'll fix you," Jenny snapped. But she did not realize that any deviation from a chance score of five may indicate the presence of ESP, whether this takes the form of hits or, as in this case, of misses. Later tests showed that Jenny could score high or low at will.

From this peak of active involvement in her own ESP, Jenny's interest appeared to diminish. Mira remembers that the child's fascination with card tests, as well as the number of incidents of spontaneous ESP, started to decline at adolescence. "Now it's boys she's interested in," Mira says. Jenny, sitting next to her on a sofa in the library, looks a little pained at this remark, but doesn't argue.

"Actually," Jenny says, "my interest has come back lately. There's an ESP testing machine that I've been working with and really enjoy."

"She's been scoring as high as twenty-three out of twenty-five," Mira adds. "Chance is six point five."

Jenny continues, "I just don't like to talk a lot about it, or to have the feeling that I have to *perform* ESP for people. I just like to do it for fun.

"My friends don't understand it, but they think it's interesting. And they don't make fun of it. One of my teachers at school sometimes makes fun—I once wrote about ESP in a paper for her class and she really didn't want to believe me—but I get back at her by saying things like, 'I'm going to dream about all your secrets,' or 'You be nice to me or I'll zap you . . .' I'm kidding, of course. I wouldn't think of using my ESP to hurt someone, even if I could. And I don't see how I could even if I wanted to."

Though Jenny is speaking seriously, there is something in her manner which makes a listener want to smile in response. It is as if some aspect of her barely hidden from view were savoring a profound but good-natured joke.

"Some of my friends even get involved in my ESP," she says. "Not long ago, I had a dream—twice the same night, in fact—that I had set my clock radio for the wrong time and it woke me up at 6:00 A.M. In the dream, I tried to go back to sleep, but couldn't. So I decided to get up and go to school to play basketball. When I got to the bus stop, my best friend, Ann, got off a crosstown bus—not the one she usually takes—and told me she was going to school to play basketball. So we both went and played. This was all in a dream, remember.

"Well, the clock radio really *did* go off at six that morning and I really did get up thinking I'd go to school and play basketball—a crazy idea because, for one thing, the school isn't even open that early. When I got to the bus stop, Ann really did get off the crosstown bus. She said she was going to school to play basketball. When we got to school, the janitor let us in and said we were lucky because he had come early to do some work. He usually didn't open up until at least an hour later."

Ann later confirmed this story, adding that she got up that morning with no real awareness of the time. She always takes the Eighty-sixth Street crosstown bus to school, she said, but, on that occasion, found herself running down to take the Seventy-ninth Street bus, which let her off at Jenny's stop.

Jenny has been sitting on the front edge of the sofa, toying with the clasp of a small locket while she talks. Now she moves back, drawing her legs under her and smoothing the skirt of her summer dress. "Another way my ESP involves my friends," she says, "is that they are always coming up to me for advice. I suppose I'm able to tune in somehow on their problems, because my suggestions to them usually work.

"For example, I have a friend who lives out of town. We have been writing to each other for years. Our mothers are very close friends. Well, more than a year ago, the girl told me she was having problems. She had matured quickly and felt very awkward and self-conscious. She was getting interested in boys, but she didn't know what to say to them. So I started giving her suggestions, things like looking at herself in the mirror every morning and saying to herself, 'You're beautiful, you're beautiful,' over and over. A lot of things like that. That may sound silly, but I think it has really worked. At least her mother thinks so. She wrote to my mother the other day and said, 'Whatever Jenny is telling her to do, I don't want her to stop. It's working.' I don't know how much ESP this involved, but I know when I read the girl's letters and try to figure out what to tell her, I seem to know things about her which I haven't been told by her or anyone else.

"This happens with people I meet, too. I can usually tell right away whether or not I'm going to like someone. It doesn't have much to do with what they do or say, it's just a feeling I get. I remember once when a relative married a woman and brought her to meet the family. My mother and just about everyone else liked her a lot. Except me. I got the feeling she was like a cat; she could be nice and 'purry,' but then she could suddenly be very cold and just walk away from you and not care. I remember everyone was surprised at my reaction, but later, after a year or so, they could see what I meant."

Jenny smiles and shrugs, as if she wants to dispel any impression she might have given that she is stuck on herself. She shows a New Yorker's matter-of-factness and self-confidence. But, by nature or design, she is able by a gesture to appear childlike, vulnerable, self-deprecating. Then, just as quickly, the poise and assurance return.

"Once in a while my ESP will get me into scary situations. I remember one time just before Mark and I were to fly to Europe and Israel with my father, his wife and some of her family, I had a terrible dream. In it, we arrived at an airport where there were lots of soldiers. Some of the soldiers came rushing up to us with a wheelchair. Somehow I knew this meant that my mother was sick and I started to cry, which woke me up, still crying. After that, I refused to leave Mother and go on the trip. I was sure she would become terribly ill if I went. But she insisted.

"Sure enough, when we got to Athens, our first stop, I recognized the airport as the one in my dream. The soldiers were there just as I had seen them. Then some of them came toward us with a wheelchair and I really flipped. I screamed that Mother was sick and started to cry. But Mark, when he could get me to listen, said the wheelchair was for our stepmother's mother, who was traveling with us. She'd just gotten tired and a little nauseated from the long flight. But for a few moments it had really given me a scare.

"I'll never forget another time when I thought I saw Nana, my mother's grandmother, after she died. I don't know if I was asleep or not, but I found myself with her, playing Scrabble. She didn't look dead at all; she looked very, very healthy and happy. I remember she had a pretty robe on her lap that was green, brown, and white with roses on it. The whole scene was so *real*. At one point, she said she had a message for me to give to my mother. 'Tell her, "Sugarplum," ' she said.

"Well, when I realized what was going on, when I woke up or whatever, I was really scared and ran crying to Mother. I described the robe on Nana's lap and she just about dropped. She told me Nana had made a robe for Aunt Addy while I was away at camp. It was green, brown, and white with roses on it! I had never seen it before.

"And when I mentioned that Nana had said the word 'Sugarplum,' she was *really* amazed. That is what Nana had called her when she was a baby, but the name hadn't been used for many years. In fact, Mother had almost forgotten it, and Grandma, when Mother asked her about it, *had* forgotten. It's possible one of them might have mentioned it to me, but they don't think so.

"I don't think I'm afraid of death, but this experience really shook me, so I prayed to Nana that it wouldn't happen again. And it didn't. Later, I prayed to her about other things; like, one time, the answer on a math quiz. She had always been good at arithmetic. It was an advanced question at the end of the test that we could try to answer for extra credit. I didn't have a clue about how to do it, but I needed the points. So I said, 'Nana, please help me.' All of a sudden the answer popped into my head. It was as if there was a dark screen inside my head and I could see the answer written in white lettering. And the answer was right! The teacher was amazed because I hadn't done any calculation. But he knew I couldn't have copied it from anyone because no one else in the class got it."

Mira adds, "It always interests me when Jenny talks about praying in these ESP situations. In purely parapsychological terms, there's no way of knowing what this means or what effect it has. The only thing I can say is that it has some catalytic influence and that Jenny somehow knows this and just uses it spontaneously. It's really something she has developed on her own.

"As a family, we're not religious in the sense of observing all the traditional practices of our faith. But I've always felt that Jenny was born knowing God. It's really a wide open faith she has, entirely her own and not the result of coaching by me or any other member of the family. I remember one day Jenny came home from school feeling horrible. So I put her to bed and took her temperature, which was one hundred and two. I told her she was going to have to stay home from school the next day, maybe a few days after that. She was furious. 'What do you mean I have to stay home?' she said. 'I've got lots of things I need to do at school.' But I was firm with her. So she said, 'What if I *didn't* have a temperature? Could I go?' And I said, 'The point is you *do* have a temperature. Let's not argue about it.'

"Well, Jenny doesn't give up easily. About fifteen minutes later, she called me to her room and asked me to take her temperature again. Now, there was no aspirin in her room, which might have made her temperature go down. And she swore to me she hadn't taken any. Besides, I had not been out of the room long enough for aspirin to take effect. At any rate, I took her temperature, staying in the room just as I had before. It was normal. I took it again. It was still normal. What could I do? The next day she went to school.

"About a week later, when I was saying good-night to her, she said to me, 'Do you remember the day I had a temperature and it went down? I prayed to Jesus because he was a healer. Was that O.K.?'

"She did a similar thing later at summer camp. I wasn't there, but the camp nurse reported that her temperature had gone down quickly when Jenny learned that she might have to stay in the infirmary. We know that people with biofeedback training can do this and that yogis can too, but it's interesting that a little girl can do it with prayer."

Jenny squirms. "Mother, I'm small, maybe—so are you—but I'm not *little*."

"I was thinking about you *then*, dear, meaning several years ago. O.K.?" Mira continues, "Maybe I should add this incident, too. I don't want to sound like a doting mother, but I think it says something interesting about Jenny.

"You remember I said that our family is not especially religious. We do have a deep sense of our cultural and spiritual traditions, I think, but this doesn't carry over into going to temple all the time. It was a surprise, then, when Jenny told us that she wanted a *bas mitzvah,* which corresponds to a boy's *bar mitzvah*. Well, we'd been through it with Mark and told Jenny she would have a lot of studying and memorizing to do—which, despite her good grades, is just not her cup of tea. But she didn't seem fazed by this, so we went ahead and arranged everything.

"I got more and more worried as the date of the ceremony drew near. Jenny was taking the whole thing very seriously— very reverently, I should say—but she just didn't seem to be studying. I kept having visions of her forgetting everything and being disgraced in front of all our friends and family. By the day of the *bas mitzvah* I was a wreck. It didn't help *at all* when Jenny kept telling me not to worry.

"Now, this may sound strange, but when Jenny stood in front of everyone to do her recitation, she became someone else. She wasn't my child. I have never heard anyone, young or old, speak of spiritual matters with such authority. I wasn't the only one to react this way. People came up to me after the service, some with tears in their eyes, and told me that Jenny had given them the most profound religious experience of their lives. Now, what do you make of that?

"I don't want to imply she's some kind of saint. She's hardly that. But she always rises to the occasion, she always seems to be able to do the right thing in a difficult situation. Usually, of course, this happens in small ways and you have to be alert to notice. Just last Saturday, for example, the foundation I'm running sponsored a large symposium. Friday night we had some of the main participants here. Saturday morning, I had to leave for

39

the conference center at 6:00 A.M., so there was no chance for me to clean up. When the symposium was over, somebody suggested, to my horror, that we all come back here because there would be plenty of room. What could I do? All the way over, I kept apologizing that there would be filthy ashtrays, dirty plates, no food, and so on. But when we arrived, the apartment was immaculate, there were snacks prepared, a big bowl of punch, and a freshly baked cake. Jenny had done the whole thing."

"I was playing tennis that afternoon," Jenny says. "About three o'clock I got an impression, almost like a voice speaking to me, that there would be a party at the apartment later. I'm used to paying attention to these things, I guess, so I just went home and got to work."

She continues, "Like Mother says, most of my ESP seems to happen in difficult situations, when there is some kind of need and I'm feeling nervous and keyed up. Sometimes I will have the feeling that I *have* to use ESP, that I really have no choice. That's when I'm likely to pray. I don't go around thinking about God every minute, but I know He's there.

"Maybe I can explain the way I feel by telling about my experience with a Hollywood movie I was going to be in."

"A movie you tried out for," Mira corrects.

"Well, they said they wanted me to be in it, didn't they? Anyway, it was for the part of the girl in *The Exorcist* who supposedly gets possessed by some evil being, maybe the devil. The producer, who wrote the book the movie's based on, knows Mother and thought I might be good for the part. I guess he thought that if I was familiar with ESP, I wouldn't be upset by the idea of spirit possession.

"Mother and I were really excited about it. But then she read the book and went right to the movie people and told them to forget it. I remember sitting in the next room while she told them off. At first I thought she was mad because they had turned me down. But when she told me on the way home she turned *them* down, then *I* got angry. So she read me some of the passages . . ."

"Some of the less offensive passages," Mira adds.

". . . and that *really* got me upset. Everywhere you turn— TV, movies, books—ESP is made so vulgar, as if it's something evil. I wish people would understand that it can be really beautiful. And helpful. It's not the most important thing in the world to me, but as long as I have it I use it. If I use it properly, to help people and not for selfish reasons, it's really a joyful thing. And if I misuse it, it could easily disappear.

"I know this is true. Once I did something dishonest at school and lost my ESP. In the cafeteria one day I picked up two brownies that were stuck together. When the cashier charged me for only one, I didn't say anything. It seemed like a little thing, getting a free brownie. But right away, I knew my ESP had gone. I tried everything, all the ESP things I knew how to do, but I could just feel that everything had left me. And I was too embarrassed at that point to tell the cashier what I'd done."

"I remember that day," Mira says. "When she came home, she was *miserable*."

"The next day I decided I *had* to go to the cashier and pay the dime I owed. She was so surprised by this honesty, I guess, that she said she didn't want my money. But I insisted. She probably thought I was crazy. But, sure enough, my ESP returned."

"A dime seems like such a small thing," Mira says.

Jenny turns and gazes out a window at a magnificent summer panorama of Central Park. "Well, right then a dime seemed like everything."

41

CHAPTER THREE

The Power of PK

"When I was about six," the young man told me, "I was given a watch to wear to school. It was an ordinary watch—I don't even remember the brand—but at school it started to do strange things. I would be working in class, concentrating on something, and then when I looked to see what time it was, the watch would be hours off. I was always having to pull the stem out and reset it to the right time.

"I complained to my mother. I said, 'What's wrong with my watch? It's always showing the wrong time.' She looked at it and said, 'What do you want? It shows the right time, it's running.' When I thought about it, I realized nothing happened to the watch at home, only at school. But I still didn't know what was causing it.

"Finally one day I was looking at the watch when, right before my eyes, the hands started spinning like mad. I really saw them running. Then they stopped at some hour completely different from the correct time. I think that was the first time I realized this thing was being caused by *me,* that there was something I was doing, or something about me, that made it happen. The fact that it happened at school, I guess, was because the other kids supplied some of the energy which was in some way focused through me.

"Next, I started noticing that the hands inside my watch were slightly bent. After some months passed, they bent more and more until the watch was just a joke; the little hand was so twisted that it wouldn't let the big one pass!

"There were some problems, too, with rulers. I always liked metal things and had a metal ruler. But many times I noticed the ruler was bent, so I would straighten it out. Finally, it bent in such a way I couldn't fix it, and I threw it away and got a new one. Then that one bent, too. Believe me, it was a really funny feeling to be trying to draw a straight line on paper and suddenly realize the ruler wasn't straight anymore. At last I just gave up and got a wooden ruler.

"In the beginning, when these things happened with my watch and my ruler, nobody believed me. They thought I was joking with them. Soon enough, though, the teachers began to realize something was going on around me that couldn't be explained, and the kids began to get after me to do PK for them. My reaction was to try to keep anything from happening. And I was able to do this; when I didn't want any PK it just didn't happen."

As some readers may have guessed, the narrator of this account is Uri Geller, the Israeli whose demonstrations of psychokinesis (PK) and a variety of other psi phenomena have generated widespread interest and controversy. I was in Geller's company for more than a week while he made several public appearances in Texas, and witnessed enough phenomena around him (including the bending of a ceremonial key to the city of

Houston, which curled up while still inside a sealed container) to be convinced several times over that his abilities are genuine.

Until I met Geller, however, I had looked in vain for children who could consciously influence objects without using some known implement or force. And even in Geller's case, the incidents just mentioned seem to be the extent of his early PK. Recently, seemingly as a result of Geller's notoriety, a number of children have demonstrated similar abilities. Dr. John Taylor, head of the department of mathematics at King's College, Oxford, selected and tested fifteen children among many who seemed to have picked up an ability to bend metal after watching Geller on TV. The children, aged seven to early teens, did well on Taylor's tests, which were repeated a number of times in laboratory conditions. Nonetheless, this form of PK remains a relatively isolated phenomenon to date.

Another type of PK among children that is also isolated in its occurrence but considerably better documented, historically, than the "Geller effect" is the phenomenon of the poltergeist. Meaning, literally, "noisy ghost," poltergeist is the name given to those episodes one reads about occasionally in the press when some environment, usually a private home, is beset by sudden, unexplainable noises, and objects seem to fly about by themselves.

On January 3, 1952, the Los Angeles *Herald Examiner* reported that "scientists from two universities joined a growing crowd to watch objects in a local home sneer at gravity and fly around 'like a shower of rain.' Two amazed county police officials swore that they saw Christmas cards, bottle caps, and a pin mysteriously move from one room to another in the house last night." Another Los Angeles paper, the *Times,* carried this story on December 10, 1965: "Ghostly thumpings and blasts of air in a home here have not only baffled the owners, sheriff's officers, water men, gas men, builders, and at least one college professor, but also scared the dog into moving out." In other

45

cases that made their way into the press, a water pail repeatedly tipped over and soap floated out of a soap dish in a Hartville, Missouri, home; glassware flew about in a house in Indianapolis; and the barrage of household objects was so persistent in a home in Sonora, Mexico, that the unhappy family living there was ostracized by their neighbors.

Fortunately, poltergeist phenomena tend to be intermittent and of relatively short duration, normally subsiding within a matter of weeks or months. At that point, when the strange events become markedly less frequent or cease altogether, the incident is likely to be explained away as the result of a shift in the earth below the house, or vibrations from an underground stream or tide.

Occasionally, a child is caught deliberately producing some or all of the phenomena. In the first case mentioned, the *Herald Examiner* followed its initial story with the disclosure that an eleven-year-old girl, an orphan boarding in the house in question, had admitted causing the strange events. "I did it for fun and because I like attention," she told the paper. In another instance, scientists studying a poltergeist happening in Newark, New Jersey, caught a fourteen-year-old boy throwing objects that he had earlier concealed in his shirt. And in the case I quoted from the *Times,* it was discovered that the "ghostly thumpings" that so disturbed the family dog, among others, happened only when the family's twelve-year-old son was in the house. On one occasion, in fact, an investigator saw the boy strike a closet door in his bedroom, which produced a loud noise similar to those the family had been hearing.

Whether these "noisy ghost" phenomena are produced by terrestrial aberrations or by prankish, attention-seeking youngsters, two important facts stand out: every poltergeist incident seems to include at least one individual in or near adolescence, and, second, though some children have been caught faking polter-

46

geist phenomena, they have also been carefully observed at other times when phenomena took place which they could not possibly have caused by ordinary means. For example, Raymond Bayless and Henry Gilroy, two veteran investigators of poltergeist phenomena, visited the home of the boy who produced the "booms" on the closet door of his bedroom, and witnessed the following: "At approximately 3:40 P.M. Mrs. Cannon and her children drove into the garage. They entered the house through the kitchen door and began unloading groceries. Mrs. Cannon's daughter, Dee, aged ten, walked from the kitchen through the living room and into the hallway. The girl said 'hello' as she passed us and entered the hallway where she was still in plain view of Gilroy but out of visual range of Bayless. Billy, aged twelve, entered the living room from the kitchen and walked toward the hall archway. As the boy reached a position about three feet from the hallway entrance, three violent blows sounded from the hallway. The blows were extremely loud and literally shook the house. The boy then entered his bedroom and there were no further sounds for at least ten or fifteen minutes."

The investigators concluded that, "There was not the slightest possibility for either the boy or the girl to have produced these sounds normally under the circumstances. To do so they would have had to strike the walls three times while they were in full view—an impossibility. Further, neither child so much as brushed against the wall while walking down the hall. And because, as investigators, we were eagerly awaiting the arrival of the children and hoping to witness just such phenomena as these, we were doubly alert."

Regrettably, few poltergeist cases are as conscientiously investigated as this one, but even when a child is discovered to be deliberately creating the effects, there are often episodes, particularly at the beginning of the case, when no ordinary explanation seems possible. Dr. Rex Stanford, for one, believes that as a child watches the strange and prankish goings-on which in many ways fulfill a repressed wish to be able to upset the tidy, structured, perhaps stifling adult world, he or she may enter into the excitement and seek to imitate the phenomena. At the same time, however, the child may have unwittingly caused the original phenomena he seeks to imitate.

The child's unconscious role in this, many parapsychologists say, very likely stems from a psychokinetic effect caused by the adolescent's (or near-adolescent's) repressed hostility toward one or more members of the immediate family. If people with pronounced PK ability, such as Geller, can generate at will a force that moves or alters objects with which they are not in physical contact, it is not unreasonable to assume that a child undergoing the intense physical and emotional stresses associated with adolescence might unwittingly and spontaneously produce PK. Psychiatrist Nandor Fodor, for example, has called poltergeist phenomena, "a bundle of projected repressions." Another investigator has written that, "typically, it is the unhappy, extremely frustrated boy or girl seeking an outlet for pent-up feelings and inner tensions" who is discovered at the scene of poltergeist happenings. A third calls the phenomena "a sort of unconsciously motivated and activated self-therapy, sometimes a protest against authority." And Dr. Gertrude Schmeidler has laid the cause to "repressed hostility," adding, "we all have some, after all."

A third instance in which some children seem able to create physical effects through psi involves healing. Some paranormal healing, especially when prayer is used, may also involve telepathy. But as we shall see, some children seem to be the instigators or at least the agents of psychokinetic type changes in the bodies of others.

Olga Worrall, a respected healer who lives in Maryland, began her avocation as a child in Cleveland. As far back as she can remember, she would spontaneously reach out to one of her family or to a neighbor who complained of a headache or some other pain, and, in effect, would *will* herself to make them well. She apparently succeeded so often that such cures became almost routine. "Olga," her mother would say, "come and put your hand on my forehead. I have a headache."

Once Olga's mother had a more serious problem. Sometime before, she had complained of pains in her abdomen. The doctor diagnosed a floating kidney and recommended an operation before the condition grew worse. But the mother, more concerned about her household than her own health, went about her duties until the pain became unbearable. From her bed one day she suggested to Olga that if she could cure her headaches, perhaps she could take away this pain. Olga put her hand where her mother indicated and prayed. In five minutes the pain was gone. The kidney never troubled Olga's mother again.

From Guernsey, one of the Channel Islands between France and England, comes the story of Linda Martel, who is reliably reported to have healed countless people, often by just a touch of her hand. Linda, the fifth of six children, was born August 21, 1956, suffering a variety of disorders which kept her hospitalized the first two and one half years of her life. The first sign that there was anything unusual about the girl, aside from her prolonged illness, came when she was about three months old, during one of her infrequent nights home from the hospital. The child was asleep when the father heard near her bed a sound like the wind. Just then the room was filled with a glowing light. The phenomena lasted several moments, then disappeared.

One day soon after Linda came home to stay, both parents were near her when they distinctly heard someone say, "Hello, little girl." It was a woman's voice, unfamiliar to either of them, which the father described as "lovely" and "well-educated." There was no one else in sight, and it was very unlikely, the parents said, that any of their other children, who were playing outside, could have produced the tone, the accent, or the particular location of the voice as a prank. Whether or not this event was in any way responsible, Linda's condition improved rapidly from that time on.

Shortly after this, during one of Mr. Martel's frequent migraine headaches, Linda reached out and placed her hand on his forehead. Almost immediately the pain disappeared. Since that day, the father never suffered another migraine attack.

Other cures followed, achieved, it is said, simply by her touch or by the use of a cloth which she had touched. For instance, a man who was receiving medical treatment for varicose veins applied a cloth to the affected areas of his legs. Within two days, the condition was gone. "Every word is true," the man insisted. "I had a reply from the local hospital stating my next visit to them was canceled as there was no trace of varicose veins." Spontaneous cures of such afflictions as a slipped disc, infected gums, rheumatism, ear infection, nasal blockages, and coronary disorders were also said to have been brought about by the child. All these were investigated and corroborated by the press and by Charles Graves, whose *The Legend of Linda Martel* related thirty-four cures attributed to the child that were representative of a larger number documented.

Once her ability appeared, Linda devoted most of her time to receiving the sick, for which no money was accepted. No one was turned away, although Linda, who could apparently diagnose an illness instantly, even look at a photograph and know who in it was sick, who had died, and who was still living, sometimes told visitors that she could not help them. Often when these "incurables" approached her, she would begin to cry. According to her parents, she never played with toys and did not have the usual interests of children. Nor did she ever do anything to require their punishment.

Many times Linda talked of "my Lady" and "my Jesus

Christ," who appeared often to her, she said, usually at night. This puzzled her parents, particularly the references to "my Lady." The Martels belonged to, though seldom attended, the Anglican church, which does not stress devotion to the mother of Jesus. Frequently Linda was heard conversing with someone after she had gone to bed, but she would stop talking if anyone approached her door to listen. She sometimes saw "my Lady" and "my Jesus Christ" in daytime as well, announcing their presence to friends or family who happened to be in the room and then sitting silently, her face expressing profound joy and peace. It was "my Lady" and "my Jesus Christ," not herself, she said, who performed the healing; they healed *through* her. Despite this evident piety, however, she refused to enter a church and cried in distress when she heard hymns sung.

Several weeks after her fifth birthday, Linda began to have pains in her lower back. Her parents sent for the doctor, but Linda insisted there would be nothing he could do. During the days that followed, she made a number of remarks to her parents and other relatives which they later understood to be references to her impending death. On the morning of October 10, 1961, after slightly more than five years of life, half of which she spent in a hospital, having never been able to walk, Linda Martel died in her mother's arms.

The clothes she touched apparently still have curative powers. At least this is the strong belief of a man from the Isle of Wight who suffered a coronary thrombosis in February 1968 and was forbidden by doctors to climb stairs or walk more than very short distances. He managed to obtain a piece of clothing that once belonged to Linda and wore it over his heart. At his next visit to the doctor, he was told that he was "like a new man." This seems to have been substantiated on a trip made in September 1968 to a neighboring island. The man and his wife became lost during a stroll and ended up climbing up and down a series of

51

steep steps cut into the sides of rocky cliffs, a feat that should surely have finished him. But he reported no ill effects whatever from this ordeal.

There are even reports that some people have been healed just by being near Linda Martel's grave. One case involved a resident of Guernsey who agreed, as a favor to Linda's father, to visit the grave and determine what flowers might be planted there. The man had been a gardener until a back injury which prevented him from bending over made him find other work. From the day of his visit, the man reported, "I haven't felt even a twinge in my back." Soon after, he spent a weekend digging up tree stumps. To have tried this a few weeks before, he said, "would have been wishful thinking."

It would also be wishful thinking if I pretended to understand how an ability such as Linda Martel's operates. A common opinion among skeptics is that much of this type of healing counteracts essentially psychosomatic disorders. This may be true in some cases, but it by no means explains them all—spontaneous cures in infants, for example, or in adults who had not sought healing or who were actually scornful of such matters. In any event, soon after I encountered the story of Linda Martel, I had the opportunity to meet another young healer, Monica Lopez of Mexico City, who further introduced me to a world where the miraculous seems to be an everyday occurrence.

CHAPTER FOUR

Monica

"I am sorry, señora, but your baby girl will not live."

Maria Almaraz de Lopez heard the doctor's words and felt the weary warmth of recent childbirth turn to sudden, icy despair.

"It is her pylorus," Dr. Zaporta continued. "Between her stomach and intestine there is no pyloric orifice. She is too little, too weak, for an operation. Señora, I am so sorry, but there is nothing to be done."

Señora Lopez had already been blessed with six children and a comfortable, if modest, home. Her husband, Antonio, a skilled goldsmith, held a secure and responsible position with a large state-owned firm in the center of Mexico City. But at this moment such matters offered little solace from her shock and grief.

Almost instinctively, she closed her eyes and prayed to the only real source of comfort she knew, commending to the Lord the life of her newborn baby. As she prayed, she envisioned a small

53

statue of Jesus that recently had come to occupy a prominent place in the home and in the devotions of the Lopez family.

The statue had a curious history. Some months before, Señor Lopez had been shopping for business supplies in downtown Mexico City. Passing a store that sold religious artifacts, he noticed in the window a small seated figure of Jesus. Almost without thinking, he walked into the store and bought it.

The whole family was pleased with his purchase. The statue was placed near the front door, where everyone could see it.

One day, a tiny drop resembling a tear appeared in one eye of the figurine. It was carefully wiped away, and no one thought much of it. A few days later another "tear" appeared and also was removed. When a third droplet materialized, the family began to wonder. Perplexed, Señor Lopez consulted Father Baltazar Lozada, a local church official. Under the priest's careful scrutiny, the statue continued to cry. "This is extraordinary," Father Lozada said. "It appears that God somehow wishes to favor your family."

The Lopez baby was hastily baptized and given the name Maria del Monte Carmelo Monica Lopez Almaraz. Her date of birth at Mexico City's Lourdes Hospital was May 4, 1958.

Despite the medical prognosis, Monica was still alive the next morning. Her heartbeat and other life signs were normal.

Dr. Zaporta was astounded. "It is not possible. It is *just not possible!*" he exclaimed to the night nurse as he examined the infant. No longer could he find anything wrong with her.

That day, the little statue of Jesus in the Lopez home stopped crying and has not cried since.

There were more unusual occurrences as Monica grew. One evening when she was four months old, the baby was lying in her crib, when suddenly there was the noise of a tambourine. Her parents, sitting nearby, were startled. There *was* a tambourine near the crib, but it was too far away for Monica to reach—not that she yet had the strength or co-ordination to lift it. Her parents assured each other they hadn't touched the instrument. But who had? There was no one else in the room.

Then a toy rose up, drifted over to the crib, and landed softly next to Monica. Other toys followed. The baby laughed and waved her arms while her parents stared in amazement. After the activity stopped, Señor Lopez confessed that he had seen the same thing happen another time. He hadn't told his wife because he did not want to alarm her. Señora Lopez then made a confession of her own. She, too, had seen the phenomenon before, but, for the same reason, had kept it to herself.

Another time, when Monica was four, the family was finishing dinner when Monica said she was tired and went upstairs. Fernando, the eldest son, shared the bedroom with Monica. He was due to get up early the next morning and went upstairs soon after his sister.

In a moment Fernando was back downstairs, wide-eyed and pale.

"Father! Father! Come quickly!"

Señor Lopez took the stairs two at a time. Through the partially opened door of the bedroom he caught a fleeting glimpse of the radiant form of a man, which now rapidly reduced itself to a small sphere of light above the bed where Monica slept. In a few moments, the light disappeared.

The two made their way back to the living room. "I opened the door quietly so I wouldn't wake up Monica," Fernando explained. "Then I saw this man standing at the foot of her bed, just smiling and looking at her. He was a beautiful figure, really, but I got scared and ran to get you. Who was he, Papa?"

Señor Lopez shrugged. If he had any explanation for what had happened, he did not reveal it.

On Good Friday, 1966, shortly before Monica's eighth birth-

55

day, thirty-seven relatives and friends knelt in prayer before an altar in the Lopez home in a traditional Holy Week observation.

Suddenly Monica grew pale. Her face sagged and her body began to sway. She looked as if she were about to faint. Instead, she fell to her knees. Then her mouth opened and out of it flowed a white mist which, to the complete astonishment of the others in the room, began to take on the shape of a man. At that moment, the room became suffused with a beautiful, unearthly light and the fragrance of flowers filled the air.

Everyone but Monica saw the tall, Christlike figure of light. They watched him lean over and place his right hand on Monica's head, as if in blessing.

Monica seemed very weak. As the radiant figure lingered, Señor Lopez went to his daughter's side, lifted her, and carried her to a daybed at the back of the family chapel. Moments later, the apparition began to disappear slowly, though the beautiful light and pleasant aroma remained, as did a pervasive sense of peace. It was then that something unusual was discovered on the white prayer cushion on which the radiant figure had stood. In the middle of the imprint of a foot were a smear of blood and two thorns.

News of the apparitions caused a stir in Mexico City. The local press flocked around the Lopez home, where Monica answered questions about the apparition with a maturity and sincerity that impressed reporters. They were also impressed by the testimony of two prominent citizens of Mexico City who had been present. Señor Y. de Jesus Guth, head of Mexico's petroleum distribution, and socialite Lily Lichtemberg had been in the Lopez home that day and confirmed that the events had taken place just as the Lopez family had described them.

Several days after the apparition, Monica experienced a voice —she did not so much hear it, she explained, as feel it within herself—which instructed her to "work for humanity, so that evil will cease and there will be love and peace among all." There was no question in her mind that the Lord had spoken to her.

The apparitions became an annual occurrence during Holy Week. For the first three years, only onlookers could see the radiant, Christlike figure. But then it became visible to Monica, too. On these occasions, the light which filled the room was so bright that the windows were kept covered to prevent a commotion among the crowds of people outside who could not be accommodated in the small family chapel.

Besides the blood and thorns, other objects materialized during the early apparitions. These included two coins which experts dated back to ancient Rome, and a heart-shaped stone on which was inscribed in Latin, "Glory to God in the highest; on Earth, peace, good will to men." Messages were also received by Monica clairaudiently. On several occasions, she wrote in flawless Latin, a language neither she nor any member of her family had studied.

It was soon evident that healing would be a major part of Monica's "work for humanity." As word of the Good Friday apparition circulated, simple people began to seek and receive the girl's help. One of these was a poor man named Galdino Pantaleon. He had moved from a rural community to Mexico City, where he found work. But then he suffered a ruptured appendix. An emergency operation was poorly performed and an infection resulted, subjecting him to constant pain. His absence from work caused him to lose his job. After a second operation, his condition grew still worse. Doctors did not expect him to survive. In desperation, Galdino's sister wrote to Monica and asked her to pray for him.

Immediately Galdino rallied and was soon back on his feet. He made a special trip to thank Monica. "I have been reborn," he told her tearfully.

There was also the case of Joaquina Rodriquez, who had

fallen into deep depression after her husband died. She found herself weeping almost constantly and felt helpless and without purpose. Her priest suggested that she seek spiritual help from Monica.

She took his advice. Each night before retiring, Señora Rodriquez said her customary prayers, then thought of Monica (though she had never seen her) and silently implored the child for help.

One night the widow was awakened by the touch of a cool hand on her cheek. She opened her eyes. The bedroom seemed slightly illuminated, though no lamp was lit.

Next to her bed stood a small girl, looking at her affectionately. "Don't be afraid," the child said. "Don't be afraid and don't cry. I am with you. Pray to God and pray for me." The girl raised her right hand in blessing, then vanished. The child appeared three more nights, repeating the words and the blessing given the first night.

"I do feel better," Señora Rodriquez told her priest. "I am more tranquil now, more at peace with things. And, thank God, my terrible weeping has stopped."

"Perhaps you would like to come with me to meet Monica?" the priest suggested.

The day the two visited the Lopez home, there was a crowd outside the front door. A girl stood in the doorway blessing small containers of water people brought to her. The widow recognized her immediately as the young one who had appeared to her. "Little girl!" she cried. "Little girl! You, it's you!"

Monica looked at her and smiled. "Yes," she said quietly. "Don't be afraid. I am with you. Pray to God and pray for me."

There seemed no limit to the ways Monica could help people. Some, including those like Señora Rodriquez who had never met her, found their prayers to her answered. Others, among them a young boy who had been hospitalized in a prolonged coma, responded to her touch. In the last case, Monica and her father had been visiting a government building when a parking lot attendant recognized Monica from newspaper photographs and begged her to help his son. She agreed and immediately went to the hospital. As incredulous doctors looked on, Monica put her hand on the boy's forehead. Almost at once, the boy's eyelids flickered, then opened. He was fully conscious.

Most frequently, Monica blessed water which people brought to her in containers ranging from expensive vials to pop bottles. The crowd Señora Rodriquez had seen outside the Lopez home was typical of the numbers of people who, having heard of or experienced the effect of her blessing, came to visit Monica.

The blessed water even worked for skeptics. Father Vincente, an associate of Monica's confessor, Father José Vidal Medina, would have been the last person to wait outside Monica's house with a container of water. To him it was all foolishness. "Perhaps the little one is sincere," he told Father Medina, "but this is all the superstition of simple people. It is all trickery on someone's part, I assure you."

To prove his point, Father Vincente put the water to a severe test. In his parish was an appealing young child named Angeles Ortiz, who had been born mute. When Angeles was four, her parents had sold their small plot of land and moved to Mexico City in the remote hope that specialists could cure her defect. But after three operations which cost the parents everything they had, Angeles still couldn't talk.

"Get me some of that water," Father Vincente said to Father Medina. "If it works for little Angeles, I'll believe. That will make two miracles at once: Angeles will speak and I will believe all this nonsense!"

He took the water to the Ortiz home.

Two hours later José Ortiz was at the rectory door. "Father, Father, my daughter speaks!"

Father Vincente forgot his dignity and ran with Señor Ortiz to the house. There he found Angeles repeating again and again, "I . . . can . . . talk! Papa, Mamma, I . . . can . . . talk!"

But as soon as one skeptic was convinced, there was always another.

One day Monica went to a Franciscan church and was recognized by a priest there. "You are the little girl associated with the apparition everyone speaks about, are you not?"

"Yes, Father."

"Some say it was an apparition of our Lord. Is this correct?"

"Yes, those who were there say that."

"What do *you* say?"

"I did not see him, Father, but I felt his presence."

"You say God spoke to you?"

"Yes, Father."

"And then you began to heal people with water, and so on?"

"Father, I do not do these things. They are done *through* me."

The priest shook his finger. "Child, this is a serious matter. If you are deceiving people the Lord will be very severe with you. On the other hand, if what is claimed is real, I wish you to perform something here. Right at this moment!"

Several adults who knew Monica heard this exchange and tried to explain to the priest that such prodigies did not happen simply because someone wanted them to. Monica was an instrument of a high will, they said. It was not up to her to determine when and where something miraculous would happen.

The priest was not moved. "You are making excuses for her," he said. "You may believe if you wish, but I have seen nothing to convince me."

A while later, during Mass, the skeptical priest was elevating the wine when a small cloud seemed to form just above the chalice. Just then he heard Monica, some distance away, say to him, "Father, He has given you your proof."

There on the altar, a piece of eucharistic bread had instantly materialized.

During the morning of September 28, 1972, five unexpected visitors came to the office of Señor Lopez at the large, state-operated business where he worked. There were two couples who appeared to be in their twenties and a child not yet two.

"Señor Lopez?"

"Yes. Please come in."

The visitors looked a little stunned. "You *are* Señor Lopez, Antonio Lopez?"

"Why, yes. Why do you seem so surprised?"

"Well, we thought it would be much more difficult to find you."

The young man speaking had a pleasant face and a quiet, self-assured manner. He spoke excellent Spanish with only a trace of a foreign accent. "You see, we just now arrived in Mexico City and we were prepared to spend days looking . . ."

"For Monica?"

"Yes."

"How did you know to come here?"

"Through friends of ours in the U.S. We're from New York."

"I see." Señor Lopez, a stout, affable man, smiled broadly. He seemed to be enjoying some private joke which he was now going to share with his visitors. "Well, you may be more fortunate than you realize. Not only did you find me, but the person you are really looking for happens to be here, too."

Monica had been in another part of the room when the visitors entered, but now, as her father beckoned, she came over and greeted them.

To the Americans she appeared surprisingly small, perhaps

several inches under five feet. But somehow she seemed very strong and remarkably poised.

Señor Lopez explained that these people were from New York and had come seeking her help.

"It is for the child," their spokesman added. "She is epileptic."

Monica smiled at her. "What is her name?"

"Dominica."

"And yours?"

"Oh, excuse me. My name is Steven, Esteban. These are Dominica's parents, Paul and Karen, and this is my friend, Alice."

Monica smiled and nodded at each. "Did you bring some water?" she asked.

"I'm afraid we didn't. We weren't expecting to find you so soon."

"No matter," said Señor Lopez. "We will find something."

Monica disappeared into a back room and returned with a Coca-Cola bottle, which she filled from a tap. Then, holding the bottle in her left hand, she raised her right hand over it, her first two fingers extended. She concentrated, then made the sign of the cross three times. Monica handed the bottle to Karen, who offered it to Dominica.

It was a moment Karen and her husband had waited many months for. Their eyes met for an instant, then both parents looked at their small blond daughter as she drank the blessed water. They could remember the nightmarish days less than a year ago when Dominica began to have her seizures, sometimes many per day. At first they did not know what was wrong, but then the realization came to Karen: her own sister had suffered *grand mal* epilepsy almost all her life, and the symptoms were disturbingly similar.

Doctors confirmed epilepsy and prescribed phenobarbital. When this did not control the seizures, they increased the dosage, still without the desired effect. Then Dilantin was given, but this produced an adverse reaction.

Dominica's parents began to feel desperate. They worried about possible side effects from the anticonvulsant drugs and became further alarmed when, despite steadily increasing dosages, the convulsions continued.

At that point, they heard of Monica from friends in Texas. The friends, editors of a research journal, had come across several articles about Monica but had never met her. However, from descriptions of her life and her attitude toward her ability, she seemed to them to have a genuine gift.

The prospect of traveling to Mexico City from upstate New York loomed as a long, costly, and uncertain project. They did not even have Monica's address. The editors had mailed them an old newspaper clipping which mentioned her father's place of business, but there was no guarantee he still worked there. When Dominica's condition continued unimproved under medication, however, they decided to take a chance. Steve and his friend Alice agreed to accompany them on the drive.

On their way, the travelers visited their friends in Texas and agreed to call if and when they located Monica. Several days later, Steve telephoned the good news that they had found her, and the editors flew down to join them.

"We've been to Monica's house twice since we first went to her father's office," Steve told the new arrivals. "She sees people every afternoon after school, except Thursdays and Sundays, when she goes to the country with her family."

"Their home is such a calm place," Karen added. "There are children everywhere—she's the seventh of ten, you know—but they get along beautifully. We have never heard any arguments, any voice raised. Even when we arrive there feeling hassled by the Mexico City traffic, we begin to feel peaceful almost immediately."

Close to 5:00 P.M. the group parked in a modern shopping complex in a residential area not far from the University of Mexico. A short walk took them to a row of well-kept houses sequestered behind high walls and iron gates. They stopped before one high, sheet-iron gate and pulled the bell rope.

A door in the gate opened and a girl's face peered through. She smiled, opened the door, and the visitors filed into a small courtyard where two small children were quietly playing. Dominica wiggled out of her mother's arms and joined them.

The group now entered a one-story structure which ran the length of the courtyard from the street to the house. Inside was a small chapel, perhaps twenty feet long and ten feet wide. At the end nearer the house was an altar, before which stood a table, a prayer desk, and, further back, eight small chairs arranged in a semicircle. Almost every surface bore some kind of religious painting, statue, or other memento, including a painting and a painted wood carving of Jesus crucified, and a small photo of Monica in ecstasy on Good Friday. Inconspicuously displayed near the back of the chapel were medals given in gratitude for healing received through Monica, and a number of crutches, apparently no longer needed. Nearby a small sign informed visitors that Monica and her family would accept no payment of any kind.

As the visitors glanced about, they almost overlooked a very small pair of corrective shoes attached to leg braces of metal and leather. Judging from their size, they had once been used by a child of two or three. The tiny apparatus, unlaced and unbuckled, stood against the wall like an opened cage, their former occupant now free.

The editors had been so preoccupied with the surroundings that for a moment they were unaware that a young girl had entered the chapel. She was small but sturdy, dressed in a light pink blouse and tan trousers, and stood facing them in a slightly boyish posture, feet apart, hands in her hip pockets. Though she was smaller than they had anticipated and her face was more finely featured than it appeared in photographs, the editors knew instantly that the young girl before them was Monica.

Steve introduced them, explaining that these were journalists and researchers who would like to ask her a few questions.

"*Cómo no?*" Monica said. "Of course."

But first, would she be willing to bless some water for them?

Again, with a smile, "*Cómo no?*"

The editors handed Monica bottles of water they had brought from home. Monica placed the containers on the table in front of the altar and quickly removed their tops. From the moment Monica had been given the bottles, she became very intent on them. Now, as she raised her right hand to bless the water, she seemed to concentrate further, as if fusing the water with her own being. Then she made the sign of the cross three times over each while whispering a prayer.

"While she was preparing to bless the water," one of the Texans said later, "I became aware of her hands, which seemed very unusual. In fact I have never seen hands shaped quite like hers. If I had seen them alone, I could not tell you if they belonged to a girl or a boy.

"As I watched her hands, I got the feeling that they were almost translucent, glowing with light from within. Then, as she made her sign over the top of each bottle, it seemed to me as if a giant spotlight suddenly had been turned on that container. I had the feeling that every molecule of that water was absolutely charged with light.

"It wasn't until several days later," he added, "that something occurred to me: I have a very strong grip and usually I put lids on so tightly that I can't open them without beating on them. I had put the lid of my water jar on extremely tightly because it was traveling in my briefcase with a lot of precious gear, includ-

65

ing cameras. It would have been a real struggle for me to get that lid open, but Monica just put her hand on it and opened it. There was no apparent effort at all. I guarantee that that lid had been sealed like a bank vault!"

Monica returned the containers and silently awaited her visitors' questions.

One editor began by briefly describing auras and asked if she saw them around people.

"No, I don't think so, though I do see a beautiful light when the Lord appears during Holy Week."

"What does the apparition of the Lord look like?"

"He is tall." She indicated a height exceeding six feet. "His hair is a chestnut color, parted in the middle, and he has a prominent nose."

"Do you have trouble with skeptics? Are there people who make fun of you at school or in the street?"

"No."

"Well, does your work, do your gifts, cause you any difficulties?"

"No. It only troubles me to see people who are sick."

At that moment, two elderly women came into the chapel with water to be blessed. They recognized five of the Americans from past days and chatted with them through Steve. Monica excused herself to attend to them.

When Monica was ready for more questions, she was urged to sit down, but she said she preferred to stand.

She was next asked whether she interpreted her dreams.

"No. Once the Virgin of San José appeared to me in a dream when I was seven. And another time I saw a long line of sick people in front of me; I remember the nearest person had a face covered with sores. I told them not to worry. But that is all. Dreams like these have a meaning for me, but I don't try to interpret the ones that aren't very clear."

"How about the future? Do you have any plans yet?"

Monica smiled and looked for a moment at the floor. It was evidently a familiar question.

"Many have asked me—usually in an encouraging way, you know—if I am going to become a nun. But I don't think it is necessary to deny oneself to that degree. I'm studying chemistry and will probably go on with this when I enter the next grade in a few months. But, you know, it is a matter of God's will. I will do whatever I feel or am told is right for me to do."

"One last question for now. Some of the young people we have talked to who seem to have unusual abilities or experiences find that their biggest difficulty comes from adults who don't understand what these abilities are or who think there is something wrong with them. What would you say to these adults?"

Monica shrugged. "Well, they should be happy there are such children."

It was obvious from such disarmingly simple answers that many of the questions which had previously been asked various psychically gifted children were just not relevant in Monica's case. What might be considered problems by most people either did not exist for her or else she accepted them as a necessary aspect of her life's work.

The Americans had been in the chapel more than a half hour and did not want to take more of Monica's time. The four with Dominica would begin the drive back to New York the next morning and began to say good-by. Steve explained that the two editors wished to come again the next day, to which Monica quickly agreed. She suggested that they come in the evening, when they also could talk with her father.

It was an emotional parting for the New Yorkers. Karen, holding Dominica, looked at Monica for a long moment, perhaps marshaling her few words of Spanish. What she finally managed to say was simply *"gracias,"* though her eyes expressed

67

a great deal more. Monica seemed moved, yet showed no strong outward emotion.

The next day, the two editors from Texas received some firsthand evidence of the efficacy of the water blessed by Monica. All morning and for most of the afternoon they went from museum to museum and art gallery to art gallery for what seemed a pleasant but physically exhausting eternity. Near the end of the day, finding themselves a considerable distance from their hotel, they tried unsuccessfully to find a taxi and were obliged to retrace their long, meandering route on foot. For one of them, such a hike should have been impossible. An old condition which periodically bothered him had, in recent days, made it painful for him to walk more than a mile or two. But that day, having taken some of the blessed water the night before, he covered well over ten miles on foot with no difficulty other than slightly sore feet. The condition has not troubled him since.

The two returned to Monica's house at eight that evening, accompanied by a young driver-interpreter hired from a sightseeing agency. The driver, cheerful and intelligent, thought he had heard of Monica but was not sure. "I am afraid I am not religious," he said, "so I really do not follow such matters."

As one of Monica's sisters led them into the chapel, they caught a glimpse inside the Lopez home through the front door. Two young children playing quietly on the floor turned bright, well-scrubbed faces toward them. Their surroundings seemed clean, comfortable, and unpretentious.

Shortly, Monica and her father came into the chapel. Señor Lopez extended his greeting with a cordial torrent of words. He was a compact, energetic man in a well-cut three-piece gray suit, black shirt, and gray tie. As he talked, it became evident that he had an immense and almost childlike enthusiasm for what had happened since Monica was born.

He recounted many of the events of Monica's life, which the

interpreter, in growing astonishment, struggled to translate. Most of the accounts the editors had heard or read about before, though in several instances the facts Señor Lopez added to what they already knew made them more plausible. For example, Angeles, the mute child who was able to speak after taking the blessed water, was reported by the press to have also been deaf. "That is not so," Señor Lopez said. "She could hear before but not speak. It could well have been psychosomatic," he added. "I cannot prove that it was really the water which healed little Angeles. But that is not important, is it? She was able to speak at last, and that is enough."

There were other cases, which the visitors heard for the first time.

"Not many days ago," Señor Lopez said, "we had three visitors from Italy—Milan, I believe—a pianist and an opera singer, both women, and a male journalist. The musicians had certain chronic illnesses. They were healthy enough to travel, but were always bothered by these disorders which the doctors could not cure. The journalist came along to observe.

"Well, while they were here, one woman said that her symptoms had gone, and a few days after they left, we received a card saying that the other began feeling better during the journey home.

"Mentioning the Italian journalist," Señor Lopez continued, "reminds me of the time a publication here in Mexico City once assigned three men to stand outside our house until they discovered us doing something bad, like accepting money from people or . . . well, I don't know what they expected to find. They were out there day after day. Of course, nothing happened—nothing they were looking for, anyway.

"Then one afternoon Monica was coming home from school when they saw her levitate, like she was walking on some invisible bridge. She just walked past them in the air. The funny thing

69

is that Monica was unaware it was happening, but they swore they saw it. So their negative story about her became a positive one.

"Something else like this happened not too long ago. A woman came here one day and told my wife that she had cancer and wanted Monica to help her. My wife said Monica was studying for examinations and asked her to please come back in a few days. Well, the woman did come back, but to thank Monica, not to ask her help. We were puzzled, of course. 'What do you mean, you want to thank her for helping you?' we said. 'You came the other day and Monica was not here.' The woman said, 'But Monica came to *me!* I saw her. I have no more pain, and the doctors say I have no more cancer.' "

Señor Lopez shrugged. "What can I say? None of this surprises us because it happens so often, the healing and also the bilocation. Monica was studying and we knew she was here. At least *this* Monica was!"

He gestured toward his daughter, who smiled slightly. No doubt she had heard stories like these countless times, but she seemed neither bored nor impatient. It was evident she was listening, but from the absence of any pride on her face, her father might have been talking of some other child, who lived in another time or place.

The interpreter asked if Monica's healing had been scientifically investigated.

"Yes," her father replied. "Though we try to make it clear that the healing happens *through* her, and is not done *by* her. You understand the difference? Anyway, three scientists from the university—it is nearby, you know—studied her quite closely several years ago. They were a psychologist, an anthropologist, and a doctor on the faculty of medicine. They watched things very closely and asked many, many questions. Their report said they

70

could find no signs of fraud in Monica or the rest of our family, and could not explain, scientifically, what they had witnessed.

"You know, it was nice to have this support from them, and for a while I thought our family should also be 'scientific' and write down everything that happens. But there is so much of it. Besides, I asked myself, what would be the purpose? It is the people's faith that is important, not a lot of evidence."

He was asked what changes Monica had brought into his life.

"Oh, many. I suppose you could say I was religious before she was born. But I am much more careful now in what I do and say. I try to have a purer life, in other words. But I am not fanatical about it. We watch television and dance; we don't want to go too far in prohibitions on the children."

"Does the rest of the family adjust well to Monica's presence?"

"Very well. She is the seventh of our ten children, seven girls and three boys. But we all pay attention to what she says. And we all try to be part of the work she does. We all try to understand the problems of the people who come here and to help as best we can.

"Besides, I'll tell you something. We all love to go into her room at night. When she sleeps there is always the wonderful odor of roses."

"Are you sometimes overwhelmed by the numbers of people who come here or write?"

"No. Monica finds time. But since we moved to this house, we have slightly fewer visitors. Still, we get thousands of cards and letters. Monica reads them, but I am afraid it is impossible for her to answer all. She puts them on the altar here and prays over them."

There was a pause. A breeze had blown open the chapel door and a family cat bounded in. Monica picked it up gently, placed

71

it outside, and closed the door. Everyone laughed as a paw poked defiantly through a space beneath the door.

It was midnight when the visitors said good-by. They shook hands and exchanged a few final words with Señor Lopez. Then Monica stepped forward and gave them each a surprisingly powerful handshake which communicated far better than words a sense of strong and enduring friendship.

Two years later, Steve, one of the group that had taken little Dominica to see Monica, returned to Mexico City for another visit. Though Monica looked older, he said, she seemed the same remarkable person he remembered. She told him that her study of chemistry had evolved into a premedical course, and she expected to be a doctor in six years. In addition to her schoolwork and receiving the sick who came to her, she participated in a group, started with some school friends, that sought to provide a spiritual environment for their contemporaries. "Unfortunately, there is not enough spiritual teaching in the home," she told Steve, "so our group is available for those who feel they need it."

To Steve's surprise, Monica remembered many details of his visit in 1972, including much of what she had said to him and his friends. She was eager for news of the others and particularly interested to know the condition of little Dominica.

Steve had brought a recent photo of the child. He also brought the news that since drinking the water in the office of Señor Lopez more than two years before, there had been no recurrence of Dominica's epileptic seizures. Monica, looking at the smiling child in the snapshot, seemed pleased but not at all surprised.

CHAPTER FIVE

Glimpses Beyond Time: Premonitions and Recollections

Several years ago, a sixth-grader I will call Dan was given an important job to do in his classroom. At the sound of the school fire alarm—whether for a fire drill or a real fire—Dan was to leave his desk quickly and close all the windows in time to follow the other children out of the room. Dan was a conscientious youngster, yet a day came when his teacher wondered if Dan was not a bit too dedicated to this new responsibility: out of the blue and with no prompting from the alarm, Dan suddenly popped out of his seat and closed all the windows. The children's laughter and the teacher's protests appeared not to bother him; he finished his job, then waited for his classmates to file out of the room. When at last the teacher convinced Dan that no alarm had sounded and that no fire drill was anticipated, the boy dutifully opened each window. But no sooner was the last window open than the alarm *did* sound for a surprise drill.

Precognition—accurate impressions of future events—seems to thread its way through much of the psi that children manifest. We have seen it earlier in Jenny's dream of the birthday party, in her premonitions of an auto accident and her step-grandmother's illness, and in her unwitting prediction of the sequence of cards in a Zener deck. And in this and subsequent chapters we will encounter premonitions which range from the relatively trivial to prophecies that, if we can give them any credence, could profoundly affect all our lives.

A significant number of children's premonitions relate to the well-being of the percipient or his family. In some cases, children's intuitions have averted injury or possible death. A dramatic example of this is the account by Mrs. Phyllis Morris, an Englishwoman, of her harrowing escape from Singapore during World War II in the company of her two small children.

"Word came that we could fly to Australia or India," Mrs. Morris recalled, "but when we approached the plane for the final check-in, my little girl started to cry and, looking at the plane said, 'No, *no,* Mummy, don't go up in alleoplane. Alleoplane go bomb, bomb, and fall in the water.' My child kept crying and pulling me to come away. Then another woman came up who was seriously ill, and begged me to give her a place. Reluctantly I relinquished my place.

"Next day we were ordered to board a ship for India. As we reached the dock and started to go up the gangplank, Diana looked around and said, 'No, Mummy, this boat not go to Auntie Lallie in India; this boat go down in water, go bomb, bomb.' I was desperate. Then my little boy looked up and said firmly, 'Oh, please Mummy, go on another boat, not this bad boat.'

Once again I returned to the flat with the predominant thought that I must get out before we were all bombed.

"In a few days we had another boat, this time bound for Australia. As we mounted the gangplank the children laughed and said, 'Oh, Mummy, nice boat go to Auntie Mary and all my other aunties. No bad bomb, bombs.'

"This time I did not know what to think, but after ten days we reached Java, where we transferred to another ship bound for Australia. We were attacked several times, but received no hits and reached Adelaide safely. Later we went to Sydney. On arrival, one of the first people we met was Aunt Mary. We heard that the plane bound for India had crashed, and all on board lost. The ship bound for India had been sunk off Ceylon, and many lives lost."

More recent and certainly more commonplace is the experience of a fourteen-year-old Brooklyn girl who dreamed of an accident involving the family car. She awoke with a strong impression that, to avoid serious injury on the next trip, her mother should sit in the back of the car. The next day, the collision took place exactly as foreseen, including the location of the accident and the general appearance of the other auto. The girl had been sitting in the front seat normally occupied by her mother and received only a minor injury. The mother, sitting in the back, was unhurt.

Unfortunately, such instances in which premonitions help avert or mitigate unfortunate incidents appear to be few. An examination by Dr. Louisa Rhine of 191 cases in which efforts were made to influence the outcome of foreseen events revealed that only nine such attempts were successful. In *Hidden Channels of the Mind* she related the tragedy of a ten-year-old boy who told his mother one morning, "Oh, Mom, I had a terrible dream last night. A car ran me down. It was so awful."

"My first thought," the mother said, "was to keep him home.

I realized I had to be calm, although my heart was racing with fear. I said that we could not live by dreams or we live a life of horror. When he left, I uttered a silent prayer and told him to stay on the sidewalk, which he did, as he was a very obedient child. Some three minutes later, someone came running to me. A truck had run up on the sidewalk and struck him down. He died seventy minutes later."

The 1966 disaster in the Welsh coal mining town of Aberfan, when a school was buried beneath a landslide, was foreseen by so many people in Great Britain that a "premonitions registry" was later established in the hope that a sufficient number of warnings concerning some future event would prompt authorities to act to prevent or lessen disaster.

One forecast of the tragedy came from an Aberfan schoolgirl named Eryl Mai Jones. "She was an attractive girl, not given to imagination," a local minister said in a story verified by her parents. "A fortnight before the disaster she said to her mother, 'Mummy, I'm not afraid to die.' Her mother replied, 'Why do you think of dying, and you so young; do you want a lollipop?' 'No,' she said, 'but I shall be with Peter and June' (her schoolmates). The day before the disaster she said to her mother, 'Mummy, let me tell you about my dream last night.' Her mother answered gently, 'Darling, I've no time now. Tell me again later.' The child replied, 'No, Mummy, you *must* listen. I dreamt I went to school and there was no school there. Something black had come down all over it!' The next day, off to school went her daughter as happy as ever. In the communal grave she was buried with Peter on one side and June on the other."

Some children's premonitions seem to have quite a different orientation, not warning of impending events, but offering guidance or reassurance for the years ahead. One such case was reported to me by Michael Wilson, an engineer who lives in

Seaford, Delaware. "When I was about seven," he said, "I had what seemed to be a long, involved, and detailed dream about the future. In the dream I seemed to be part of what I was doing, but at the same time I was discussing the events with a 'narrator.' In some scenes I was doing higher mathematics of seemingly impossible complexity, which alarmed me because I was a mediocre math student at the time. However, I was assured [by the dream] that, although there would be difficulties, all would be well finally.

"I also saw myself working around aircraft in a black hangar, yet I was not all that happy. This was a heresy because, at age seven and for years afterwards (well into my thirties), my abiding interest was *airplanes*. For me to be less than enthusiastic around them was unthinkable. I also saw another hangar, different in color and shape, just sitting there in the pale sunshine. Then many scenes of the future seemed to come and go, many of them frightening to a seven-year-old without much confidence. However, throughout the dream there was impressed on me the feeling that all would be well, that I should not worry. I awoke with a feeling of well-being, that all the events I had witnessed would turn out all right.

"Years later I was an aircraft mechanic in the R.A.F. in England. One routine day I was standing in a hangar and, as I looked across at another hangar, the black hangar of my dream was there in front of me. And several years after that, while I was working at a summer job at an airfield in Delaware, I was assigned some work one day in a distant hangar I had not seen before. When I drove up to it, I saw that it was the other hangar in my dream, sitting in the pale light.

"In college and graduate school, I was much involved with higher mathematics, which, for me, was hard work. Many times I despaired of ever passing the more difficult courses, but always

77

that feeling of 'just hold on and all will be well' seemed to return to me, just as in the dream. And all *was* well."

If it was possible for Michael to glimpse decades into his future, it should not be too difficult to accept the possibility that psi may also operate in the other direction, that children may have valid paranormal impressions of the past. The English writer Joan Grant, at age twelve, described to her parents the wallpaper in a room she occupied as an infant. The parents were incredulous, since the family had occupied the house only briefly when Joan was six months old. But they were also intrigued; Joan's father made a visit to the house and discreetly peeled back two layers of wallpaper put up in Joan's former bedroom by later occupants. Underneath he found the exact pattern his daughter had described.

There can be some question as to whether such a recollection constitutes psi or is simply an example of acute memory. However, this is but one of a number of vivid memories Joan had that not only encompassed her earliest childhood, but extended far beyond that, into what, to her, were quite obviously her earlier lifetimes. A trip to the seashore when an infant, for example, prompted in her a memory of a life as a runner who often sprinted along the sands of another shore. Joan recalls weeping in frustration, unable to make her awkward infant's body move with anything resembling the athlete's speed and grace.

The idea of reincarnation, of some human component surviving and evolving through a succession of physical embodiments, is generally alien to Western minds, though there are many notable exceptions. Thoreau wrote, "As far back as I can remember I have unconsciously referred to the experience of a previous state of existence." Flaubert told fellow novelist George Sand, "It seems to me that I have always existed! I see myself in the different ages of history, quite clearly, engaging in different trades and experiencing various fortunes." And Schopenhauer was so certain of reincarnation that he declared, "Were an Asiatic to ask me for a definition of Europe, I should be forced to answer him: It is that part of the world which is haunted by the incredible delusion that man was created out of nothing, and that his present birth is his first entrance into life." Many other Westerners, both famous and obscure, have either firmly believed in reincarnation or have seen in it a reasonable explanation for the puzzling vicissitudes of life.

For many children, though, like the young Joan Grant, reincarnation is not a matter of belief or intellectual choice, but an unavoidable fact of existence—and not always a pleasant one. A Staten Island woman named Knight told me that her daughter, then two and one half, was playing on the kitchen floor one day when she suddenly looked up and asked, "Where is my mother?" When Mrs. Knight replied that *she* was her mother, the girl protested, "No! No! I mean my *real* mother!" A bit perplexed, Mrs. Knight again assured her daughter that she was really her mother, but when this appeared to have no effect, she asked what this "real" mother's name was, thinking the girl might have in mind a grandmother or some other female relative. But the name the child gave was one Mrs. Knight had never heard. "It was an Indian-sounding name," she told me, perhaps "Shasti" or "Vashti." Her reaction to this was to tell the girl to stop her silly nonsense and to distract her with toys.

About a month later, the child was crying and the mother picked her up to comfort her. "But she pushed herself away from me as if I were a stranger," Mrs. Knight said, "and told me that she didn't want me, she wanted her real mother, and again mentioned the same Indian name. I told her that I didn't want to hear anything like that again." That was the last time the daughter mentioned this "real" mother.

"I had been brought up with a very strict Lutheran background," Mrs. Knight added. "At that point (ten years ago) reincarnation seemed ridiculous to me. Even so, the incident was so odd that it made a very strong impression on me. Later, when I became interested in this field, I felt, and still feel, that I did my daughter a great injustice by not hearing her out."

English psychiatrist Arthur Guirdham has reported the extraordinary case of a female patient who from childhood was hounded by terrifying dreams of medieval France. Details she recalled of people, places, religious customs, architecture, and dress—climaxed by traumatic memories of being burned at the stake—fitted precisely the history of the Cathari, an obscure religious sect many of whose members were put to death during the Inquisition. The psychiatrist was able to ascertain from the few scholars familiar with the Cathari that there would have been no way for the woman, either as a child or an adult, to have obtained most of the information she gave by conventional means. Particularly impressive were a number of poems she had jotted down as a child in a language she thought to be modern French. The poems turned out to be almost identical in style and wording to certain troubadour lyrics peculiar to the region and the dates of the Cathari sect. At the time the woman, as a child, wrote her poems, the lyrics were completely unknown to modern scholars.

A more felicitous case of past-life recall was recounted to me by a teen-ager I will call Linda. A quiet, thoughtful girl, Linda talked to me in the living room of her grandparents' house in a suburb of Washington, D.C.

"When I was little," she said, "I used to describe to my mother all kinds of scenes I remembered from the past. For instance, I'd tell her about ancient Egypt—the clothes I wore, the objects around me, even how the Egyptian craftsmen used to make gold thread. This was before I could read, and I don't remember seeing any picture books on the subject. I was really lucky that my mother and her parents accepted reincarnation even before I was born, before it became kind of an 'in' thing.

"When I was nine, I got to see some of the places I remembered. My grandparents took me on a trip to Southern Europe and the Middle East. There were places we visited which I just *knew*. I would get tremendously excited—at places like Tutankhamen's tomb, for instance. There were other places where I felt depressed, especially some sites in Israel and Italy. In Israel a guide would point out a place where something was supposed to have happened, some big biblical event. But I'd know it wasn't the right spot, that the real place was somewhere else.

"Speaking of my grandparents, the ones who took me on the trip, there's a very interesting situation between my grandmother and me. I'm staying with my grandparents because there's a good school near here, better than anything near my parents' home. So, in a way, my grandmother has almost become my mother, especially because my mother has always seemed like a sister to me.

"I can remember being born in this country a number of times, but I never seemed to live very long. I was always dying in childhood. I was even sick with some blood disease *this* time. Now, my grandmother had two children: my mother and an older daughter who was a diabetic and died when she was seven; my mother was born a year before she died. I remember going through a button box of my grandmother's (I'm talking about *this* lifetime now) and picking out some red buttons and something else which I can't remember. I told my grandmother, 'Oh, these are mine! What are they doing here?' My grandmother was very surprised because the buttons had belonged to her daughter who died. She had never mentioned them or showed them to me, so it seems like a confirmation of my impressions of a time when I was her daughter, the one who died."

From Burma has come an unusual case in which a boy

claimed to remember what happened to him between death and rebirth. The boy, whose family had been Christians for several generations and were therefore not inclined to believe in reincarnation, was born with strange marks and deformities on his body. A surgeon who examined him was convinced that these abnormalities could not have been caused by a prenatal injury or any aberration in the mother's womb.

The boy recalled that in his previous life he had lived alone, guarding a considerable treasure left to him by his father. One night, robbers broke into his house, bound him with wire, and made off with the treasure. He had been tied in a crouching position and could recall the wires cutting into his hands, causing blood to drip onto his feet precisely where, in the present life, his toes were joined by a malformation of flesh. Similarly, deep lines in his palms, calves, and forehead seemed to indicate where he had been bound with the wire.

"Sometimes during the night," said a report on the case prepared by the Buddhist World Mission, "he suddenly became aware that he was looking down at a still form crouched in a corner, and wondering who it was. It was only later that he realized the body was his own, and that his consciousness was now located in a different and less substantial form.

"The rest of his recollection was confused and obscure. It seemed to him that for a long time he wandered about the scene of his former life, conscious only of a sense of loss and profound unhappiness. In this condition he appeared to have no judgment of the passage of time and was unable to say whether it lasted for days or centuries. His sense of personal identity, too, was very feeble, his thoughts revolving entirely around the events just prior to his death, and the memory of his lost treasure, which he felt a longing to regain. He seemed, he said, to have his whole existence in a single idea which was like an obsession: the loss of his wealth and his desire to recover it.

"After a long time he again became aware of living beings, and felt an attraction toward a certain young woman. He attached himself to her, following her movements, and eventually another transition was effected, in a manner he was unable to describe clearly, as the result of which he was reborn as the woman's child."

What appears to have been a more purposeful "sojourn" between incarnations has been related in the case of Alexandrina Samona, daughter of a physician in Palermo, Sicily, who died at age five. In the week following the child's death, her mother twice dreamed that Alexandrina came to her and asked her to stop mourning. "I have not left you for good," the child said. "I shall come back again, little." At that time, the mother was believed unable to have more children, but within two months she was pregnant. She gave birth to twins, one of whom was remarkably similar in appearance and temperament to Alexandrina. As far as is known, "Alexandrina II" showed no conscious recall until age ten, on the occasion of a proposed family trip to an old Norman church at Monreale. "But, Mother," the girl said when she heard the plans, "I *know* Monreale. I have seen it already!" She said this despite the fact that the family had not been there since shortly before Alexandrina's death. But the child insisted, "Don't you recall that there was a great church with a very large statue of a man, with his arms held open, on the roof? And don't you remember that we went there with a lady who had horns and that we met some little red priests in the town?" The girl's description fit the church exactly, and the parents remembered that they had made an earlier trip in the company of a woman who had come to Palermo for medical treatment of disfiguring growths on her forehead which, to a child, could have readily resembled horns. They also remembered meeting a company of red-robed priests.

If indeed there is a continuum of existence, it would seem that an awareness of it, a sense of purpose and direction as suggested by the Alexandrina Samona case, would be preferable to the dim, unhappy wanderings of the Burmese houseboy. This thought became more sharply focused in my mind when I met Ray Stanford, a man who, at a very early age, experienced in one moment a recollection of an entire succession of his past lives and grew up with some inner knowledge of where, in the future, they were leading.

CHAPTER SIX

Ray

Odem, Texas, is a small farming community along the Missouri Pacific Railroad, twenty-one miles northwest of Corpus Christi. Around it stretch flat, fertile coastal plains on which vegetables and grains grow year round.

Odem has not changed much since the June day in 1938 when Rex and Thelma Stanford became parents of identical twin boys they named Ray and Rex. Then, as now, everyone knew everyone else and lent a hand when help was needed. Thus it was not unusual that when Thelma came home from the hospital with her twins, a neighbor named Addie Smith began coming over to help her with them.

One warm morning when Ray and Rex were about four months old, Addie and Thelma were washing the boys in a tub on the kitchen table. It was Monday. Addie had been to church the day before, and as the two women worked, she talked about something the preacher had said during his sermon.

"Thelma, you know that passage in the Bible about Jesus cursing the barren fig tree? Well, the preacher said this means that a women who is barren, a woman who has a chance to have children in marriage but refuses, is in danger of hell-fire and damnation *eternally*."

If Thelma Stanford had an opinion about this, she did not express it. But one of her tiny twins, the one called Ray, who at the moment was being rinsed in a white porcelain dishpan by Addie while Thelma dried Rex, was profoundly shocked. Though just an infant, Ray seemed to know what Addie was saying. But he could not understand *why* she was saying it. "What's the *matter* here?" he thought. "What is this nonsense about eternal hell-fire and damnation? Don't they *know?* Don't they remember living before?"

At that moment Ray could see in his mind's eye many of his former lives, arrayed in his memory like beads on a string. "If I live to be a hundred," he thought, "it will only be a tiny segment of *all* my lives! The same goes for them, so why don't they *know?*" He wanted desperately to say something, to set these two women straight.

"I can remember that incident as clearly as if it happened last week," Ray Stanford says. He is now in his mid-thirties, a man of medium height with dark eyes and hair and a slender, expressive face. "I even remember the dishpan I was being bathed in. It was white with a red rim around it and a metal plug, called a 'Mendit,' stopping up a hole in the bottom. I mentioned this memory to my mother a few years ago, and she recalled the dishpan. She said she threw it away before I was six months old. So I was probably four or five months old when the incident happened.

"That was an extremely significant event in my life because I *knew* my past-life memories were true, even if I seemed to be the only person around who had them. It was this certainty I had about a continuum of existence that gave me enough faith in my own discernment, my own view of reality, to be able to accept and understand other unusual experiences I encountered later on."

During childhood Stanford was often conscious of the influences of these past lives on particular interests or stages he went through. One such influence seemed to come from a memory of Tibet, where he had known how to heal plants. When a plant was sick around the home, he would place his hands on either side of it, sensing that some revitalizing energy would be transmitted from him. If he could feel the energy being absorbed, he knew the plant would get well, but if it seemed to just roll off, he took that as a sure sign the plant was too far gone to be helped.

Several more of his lifetimes seemed to involve the healing of humans. Specifically, he remembered being a physician in the United States at a time when the lack of equipment required a certain intuitive ability to diagnose illness. When young, he was able to take someone's temperature accurately simply by placing his hand on their forehead. And he seemed to be always telling his mother when someone had heart or lung trouble, even before they knew it themselves. For example, from the day he first met a Mrs. White, his eighth-grade mathematics teacher, he seemed to know she would eventually die of cancer. She taught throughout the school year, but several years later he learned that she had become ill and left her job. Not long after that, he was told that she had died of lung cancer.

Stanford reminisces about these distant memories and their influence as if they were no more unusual than recalling the events of the last week or month. He speaks with animation and obviously enjoys the humor underlying the predicaments some of his intuitions led him into. "When I told my mother about my impressions, she used to say, 'Now, Ray, stop thinking about

87

those things. You'll drive yourself crazy!' But of course I didn't listen to her.

"Actually, I'm grateful that neither of my parents paid that much attention to the ESP I had then. I've seen too many children—and parents—with inflated egos because the child shows some kind of psychic ability, real or imagined. Without knowing it, though, my mother helped me gain confidence in my past-life perceptions by reading me stories about ancient Egypt and other cultures, which confirmed my memories. For me, I think it was the best thing she could have done.

"Also, my maternal grandmother had been quite psychic, so it was not a complete shock to my mother when my medical predictions came true. Still, I gave her some uncomfortable moments. I remember when her stepfather was dying of cancer, she would take me with her when she went to visit him, but I would refuse to go into his house. I insisted that cancer was contagious. Of course, six-year-olds aren't supposed to know about things like that, and at that time there was no scientific evidence to support me. But recently several prominent cancer researchers have said they believe certain cancers are caused and spread by virus."

Sometimes Stanford's impressions about others' illnesses were helped by glimpses of their auras. On one occasion he noticed three gray spots in the area of a woman's lungs. He had learned to not volunteer what he saw to the people concerned, but in this instance, since the woman's husband was an M.D., he decided she might appreciate the information. She was appreciative, it turned out, but her chief reaction was surprise. She knew about the spots and was astonished that Ray did. They were vestiges of a tubercular condition, she told him, and for several years had shown up on X-rays precisely where Ray had seen them.

Another past-life memory was related to medicine to the extent that it was most vividly recalled during a visit to the doctor.

Ray had been born with a circular mark on his left wrist which resembled a puncture. It puzzled the child because he seemed to remember that a nail had been driven through that wrist and he had died. At the church the Stanfords attended there were pictures and discussions of Jesus being put to death by being nailed to a cross. It seemed to Ray that the same thing had happened to him, but at a later time and in another country. However, Jesus was always represented with the nails driven through his hands.

One day when Ray was six, he was taken to the office of a Dr. Voss in Odem for shots. When his sleeve was rolled up, Ray looked at his scar and asked, "Dr. Voss, did you shoot me there?" Voss replied, "No, doctors don't give shots there." At that moment, a vivid mental image came to the child of a Roman arena where he and a number of other Christians had been put to death. It seemed to him confirmation that he had been crucified. Years later he had a detailed dream of precisely the same scene. By then he was familiar with the suggestion of a number of biblical scholars that, traditional representations notwithstanding, victims of crucifixion were nailed through the wrists, as the hands could not have supported the weight of the body.

Despite such memories, or perhaps because of them, Stanford seldom saw eye to eye with the teachings of his family's church. Just as he had been shocked, as a tiny infant, by the ideas passed along by neighbor Addie Smith, he took exception to many of the things said in church and Sunday school. In fact, having earned the enmity of his Sunday school teacher by successfully challenging him on a number of doctrinal points, Stanford one Sunday staged a wrestling match on the front lawn of the church which, as he had hoped, proved the last straw. He was asked to not come back.

No doubt some of Stanford's resistance to the narrowness of his religious upbringing came from his memory of several lives as a Hindu ascetic. Long before he ever heard the word "yoga," he could assume a number of difficult yoga postures and could swallow his tongue at will. Naturally, anything so exotic was destined to make a hit with Ray's South Texas schoolmates. In his mechanical drawing class, there was a large cabinet with grooves in the sides into which drawing boards were inserted for storage. Ray seemed to know how to "crumple himself up" so that he could fit himself into almost impossibly small openings. The class would cheer him on while drawing boards were arranged in the cabinet to make smaller and smaller openings, into which he would somehow manage to fit himself. "They were always amazed when I did this," Stanford remembers, "but I'm sure they would have been triply amazed if I had told them I'd learned to do that during previous lifetimes! In fact, considering the attitude toward reincarnation in those days, they just might have locked me in that closet."

One day a boy at school saw Ray demonstrating a yoga posture. "Why, you're a yogi!" he told him.

Stanford didn't know whether to take this as a compliment or an insult. "What's a yogi?"

"Someone who does what you're doing."

Ray went to the library to see what he could find out about these people with the strange names. There he encountered *A Search in Secret India,* by Paul Brunton, which confirmed to him many of the things he remembered. In fact, he felt like shipping out to India on the next boat. This being out of the question, he read everything he could about yoga and began to meditate.

Ray took meditation seriously, but funny things sometimes happened. It was not always easy to create the atmosphere he thought appropriate for meditation, especially with nothing more than dime-store incense available, but with enough incense burning, the shades pulled down, and the lights out, he could begin to imagine himself in some suitably mystical setting. One afternoon, as clouds of perfumed smoke were billowing through the room, Ray was startled out of his meditative state, and almost out of his wits, by a sudden croak and thump from over in the corner. It took him a few moments to realize what had happened. He had forgotten to take the parrot out of the room and all the incense had made her pass out. She was evacuated to the porch, where she lay for several days, alive but paralyzed. Eventually she recovered, but she was never quite the same after her "transcendental" experience.

There were other influences Stanford sensed were stimulated by the past, though he did not have a clear impression of the time or the place. For example, when his family drove off for a picnic but weather threatened, he would loudly implore the clouds in some unknown tongue to go away. Remarkably, the clouds did seem to be affected, which reinforced his inner conviction that, to some degree, he could influence the weather and that he had been able to do so at some time in the past.

Another carry-over from the distant past involved a concoction he called "Solium-Begolium." "It may be America's least-known sports fact," Stanford says, "and maybe the least believable, too, but, when I was about eight, I felt directly responsible for the success of two of my sports heroes, Joe Louis and the great football star from SMU, Doak Walker.

"To make Solium-Begolium I took a Halo bottle that still had a little of the shampoo left in the bottom, filled it the rest of the way up with water, and sometimes added coloring. I kept it handy during SMU games and Louis's title fights—sometimes I'd help out the local high school football team, too—and when the going got tough, I put my thumb over the opening, shook it, then took a big whiff of the 'perfume' and mentally sent energy to whomever I wanted to receive it. During really exciting moments, I'd practically pass out from hyperventilation!

"I was convinced Solium-Begolium worked. Whether it did or not, I'm sure such substances have been used in primitive magic. In ancient Indian teachings, the sense of smell is associated with the *muladhara chakra,* where the primary energy in the body is said to reside. My use of Solium-Begolium could have been an unconscious impulse to awaken and, in effect, transfer that energy."

Stanford becomes reflective for a moment. "There was evidence that others in my family had at least unconscious memories of past lives. I had two adopted older brothers who used to call my mother 'Mai' and often referred to my twin, Rex, as 'Yati.' We learned years later that these are both Indian terms, *'mai'* meaning 'mother' and 'Yati' being a proper name. And almost from the time he could talk, Rex would tease me by calling me 'Rimmon.' It was a word neither of us understood, but I felt it was a real insult. Recently, we looked this one up and found that it's a Persian word meaning 'devil.'

"But if anyone besides me had *conscious* memories of living before, I don't remember their talking about it. I doubt if many people in South Texas in the forties and fifties had ever heard of such a concept. So I just kept quiet about it. And sometimes I suffered. Often when I was an infant and a small child, I became tremendously frustrated because my body wasn't co-ordinated enough to do what I wanted it to. And I disliked the crying and screaming which I did as a baby almost in spite of myself. In fact, I remember sitting in a class at school one day, totally bored by being taught a subject I felt I knew already, and thinking, 'I'm just *not* going to go through this again! If I have to come back, I'll get an older body, maybe one that has finished school, but definitely *not* one of those nasty, screaming baby bodies!' "

There were some aspects of his psi which Ray felt safe in revealing, such as the precognitive dream he once had of a new locomotive passing through town. In Odem the Missouri Pacific tracks ran through the middle of town, about a block from the Stanfords' house. Ray and Rex would cross the tracks on their way to and from school, and would sometimes watch the trains pass—usually boxcars and gondolas pulled by black, coal-burning locomotives.

One morning Ray woke in great excitement. He had dreamed that a strange new engine had passed through Odem, headed for Corpus Christi. He told everyone who would listen that it was yellow, white, and blue with a big red eagle on the front. Instead of the usual whistle made by the old black locomotives, this new one made a long, nasal wail. It was something completely new to him. He had never seen or even imagined anything like it.

Two days after that, Ray's mother found an article in the Corpus Christi newspaper which said that a new train, the Missouri Pacific Eagle, would take a new South Texas route through Odem. A few days later, a shiny, streamlined engine passed through town which was identical to the one in Ray's dream: yellow, white, and blue with a red eagle on the front.

Something else Stanford felt free to talk about and demonstrate was a type of clairvoyance he called his "mental radar." If he had a clear idea of what an object looked like, he could invariably locate it, no matter where it was hidden. He called it mental radar because radar had just become known to the public then, and the process he used to "sweep" an area mentally until he located an object seemed to operate somewhat like it.

At Christmas, children visiting neighborhood families would come over to the Stanfords' and hide things for Ray to find. This would go on all day, but Ray always seemed able to locate whatever was hidden.

Once two skeptical boys, both sons of M.D.s, decided to prove Ray a fake. They went to one boy's house, where one got into a closet with Ray while the other, a few rooms away, carefully and quietly hid a stick of lip salve in a covered candy dish. But when they let Ray out of the closet, he went right to it.

"There was a practical use for my 'mental radar,'" Stanford adds. "When my mother misplaced something around the house, she would ask me to find it for her. I had invented a stage name for myself, 'The *Fundier*,' which I somehow thought was a French word meaning 'the finder.' I would close my eyes, raise my arms dramatically, and tell her in a deep voice, 'Don't worry, The *Fundier* will find it!' And then I'd go find whatever was missing.

"Unfortunately, this particular type of ESP later faded away, for the most part, about the time I started to give readings."

A woman's voice calls from the next room, "Now it's *my* job to find things!" It is Stanford's wife, Kitty-bo. Ray laughs.

The "readings" he has just referred to began when he was in his early twenties. Since age twenty-one he has been able to enter a meditation-induced unconscious state from which he has access to information about which he may have no conscious knowledge. These have included extensive and accurate medical diagnoses of persons unknown to him and often considerably far away, and lengthy discourses on cultural, scientific, and philo-sophical subjects. Tape recordings of Stanford's readings, more than two thousand in number, are in the process of being transcribed, indexed, and published by the Association for the Understanding of Man (A.U.M.), a nonprofit, open-member-ship organization headquartered in Austin, Texas. Stanford is employed as a research psychic by the association.

Whether or not Ray's present interests are stimulated by past-life memories, a visitor to his home finds evidence of enough avocations to occupy most individuals for several lifetimes. They include varieties of plants and birds, tanks of tropical fish, and Basenji dogs that are the object of much attention and hilarity in the household. There are collections of archaeological artifacts, unusual seashells and minerals, and quantities of photographs, journals, catalogues, and apparatus in mid-assembly that indicate an active interest in experimental science. (As a teen-ager in the pre-Sputnik era, Ray built and successfully launched several multistage rockets, which won him a state science award and an offer to study rocket engineering at the University of Texas.)

But Ray's strongest interest is obviously art. His home is filled with books and objects relating to ancient Egypt, pre-Columbian America, the Italian Renaissance, certain schools of painting in nineteenth- and twentieth-century Europe, and contemporary Indian art and handicrafts of the Southwest United States. And on the walls hang several of his own paintings in acrylic—large, colorful, innovative, impressively executed.

"I've drawn and painted just about all my life," Ray says. "It's something I've always loved to do—and something I've always known *how* to do. I never had to learn how to stretch a canvas or mix colors. The ability was just there. If I didn't feel such a commitment to the kind of work I'm doing with A.U.M., I would probably paint full-time." He pauses, gazing at a canvas he calls *To Feed a Multitude*, a dazzling semiabstract depiction of Christ dividing the loaves and fishes. The painting generates a number of strong but agreeable impressions in the viewer, among them the feeling that some primal law of physics, as yet undocumented by science, is being boldly demonstrated.

Ray is asked what he means when he talks about being committed to his research work as a psychic.

"It probably goes back to that past-life recall I had as an infant, the time I was first consciously aware of life as a continuum. When I realized that the people around me weren't aware of having lived before—in fact, I was a teen-ager before I heard of anyone else who had past-life memories—I seemed to understand that part of my life's work would be to act as a kind of catalyst so people will wake up to certain realities about themselves. It's not the concept of reincarnation, per se, that's so important; in fact, people can get badly hung up living in the past, thinking about who they were or who they might have been. In a sense it's helping people get beyond a kind of mental and even spiritual provincialism which makes them blind to who they really are and what their life's purpose is.

"There was a powerful recurring dream I had from infancy until I was about thirteen. I always experienced it at the same time in July every year. In the dream, I was outside my home when from high in the northern sky came a fantastic procession of strange air- or spacecraft. Some of the craft were enormous, made of brilliantly shining metals in an incredible variety of shapes. Others, passing closer to the ground, were smaller and painted bright, vibrant colors, and trailed beautiful multicolored streamers. None of the ships made a sound as they passed over. It was a fantastically beautiful sight. I could hear the neighbors screaming and running in and out of their houses in panic when they saw the craft, but even as an infant I felt tremendous exhilaration for hours and even days after the dream.

"Now, the dream can be interpreted a number of ways, but part of its meaning for me has been that we belong to a far larger scheme of things than any of us can imagine—than most of us *want* to imagine. There are 'other worlds,' in both a physical and spiritual sense, that we have to find out about and communicate with if we're going to survive, if we're going to evolve as a civilization and not stagnate. Like my neighbors in the dream, we all have a tendency to panic when we're confronted with something seemingly new and alien. But whoever is able to stop and look up, whoever has kept enough trust and curiosity from childhood to do this, will experience a real expansion of consciousness.

"That dream gives me goose bumps every time I think about it." Ray looks at his forearm and smiles.

He pauses. "There's one thing I forgot to mention about my past-life recall. My clearest memory is of being a medical doctor, in the lifetime just before this one. My name was Dr. Clark. I graduated from the University of Chicago and practiced in Chicago and possibly in Detroit as well. I remember that I smoked a pipe, and had stomach trouble and complications in the lower abdominal areas.

"Some years back, I checked up on this and found that there was a Dr. Clark who practiced in that area at the time I remember. Later, when I spoke about this in an interview with *Psychic* magazine, a reader wrote to say that he once met a Dr. Clark who seemed to fit my description. He said this Dr. Clark had an office at the corner of State and Randolph streets, wore a mustache and beard, and, like me, had a slight build. He had some strong convictions about the communication of diseases—which I do, too—that have since been confirmed by research.

"We checked with several medical societies and found that a Dr. James Clark, who graduated from Chicago Medical College, practiced at State and Randolph. He died a little more than three years before I was born, of uremia following a prostatectomy.

"Maybe more information about Dr. Clark will turn up in time. Some friends have suggested that I go to Chicago to investigate this further, but I don't feel it would be especially useful to do this. People will come to understand and accept reincarnation not when they are presented with a collection of facts, but when something inside them is ready to respond to the meaning, the direction, that a continuum of lifetimes suggests. When you get right down to it, my work is to help them find that meaning—and live it—whether they fully accept reincarnation or not."

CHAPTER SEVEN

Intimations of Other Worlds

> As I was climbing up the stair,
> I met a man who wasn't there.
> He wasn't there again today,
> Oh, how I wish he'd go away!*

The delightful ambivalence of this nursery rhyme illustrates the dilemma of many children whose private world is sometimes visited by beings not visible to parents, siblings, and others in the "real" world. Often these visitors are products of an active imagination, but if we can believe even a few of the thousands of cases documented in the literature of parapsychology, something quite apart from childish imagination is sometimes involved.

* Hughes Mearns, "The Psychoed"

There is Dr. Louisa Rhine's account of a two-year-old boy whose parents rented a summer cottage at the New Jersey shore. Soon after they arrived at the cottage, the boy was put into one of the bedrooms for a nap. Presently, the mother heard him say, "See man, see man." Curious, she peeked into the room and saw her son standing in his crib, smiling and pointing. This happened repeatedly during the days that followed. At times the boy would urge his parents to come meet the "man," taking one of them by the hand and leading them into the bedroom. Once there, he would point, smile, and say, "See man." At nap time they would open the door a crack and watch as he smiled and offered his toys to the invisible being. The parents could detect nothing in the room, such as the movement of light and shadow or unusual furniture shapes, that the boy might in any way construe as the figure of a man.

At the end of the month, just as the family was preparing to leave, the owner of the cottage stopped by. She introduced herself (the family had known nothing about her) and told them that this was her first visit to the cottage in a year. Her husband had loved the place, she said, and died the year before in the bedroom used by the little boy. When she met the boy, she exclaimed that her husband would have "loved this adorable baby. He was so fond of children."

Denver physician Robert Bradley reported the case of a two-and-one-half-year-old girl who was accustomed to playing in the living room while engaged in a one-sided conversation with an invisible companion she called "Uncle Joe." The child was puzzled when she learned her parents couldn't see or hear her friend. For their part, the parents shrugged off the matter as the product of a vivid imagination.

Then one evening a large, friendly dog followed the father home and he let it into the house. The dog seemed right at home and happily explored about until it came to the chair supposedly occupied by "Uncle Joe." "The dog cringed in fright," said Dr. Bradley, "its tail went down between its legs, it whined piteously and ran, scratching frantically to be let out the door, and disappeared in terror, not to be seen again."

Both incidents appear to be what parapsychologists call "visions of the dead," though "dead" hardly seems the appropriate term to describe such ostensibly animate beings as "Uncle Joe" and the man in the New Jersey beach house. Reincarnation theory (see Chapter Five) would indicate that these beings, or some aspect of them, were in transition between embodiments, perhaps, like the Burmese houseboy, attached to something they valued in their recent lives. At the very least, stories like these indicate that some component survives the death of the physical body.

One interpretation of this process has come from a young boy we will call Michael, whose father died when he was three and one half. "One morning after Michael had been ill with a bronchial cold," his mother recalled, "I awoke feeling very ill myself. I heard his first morning cough and I jumped out of bed to raise him in his cot to ease the coughing. Then I realized that I could not see anything, though my eyes were open. I tensed my elbows on the rails of the cot and just hoped it was only a passing blackout. By degrees I felt better and my sight returned. Then I saw Michael was looking at something (some*one*) at the end of his cot, with every sign of happy recognition. He turned to me and said, 'You'd have fallen down, Mother, if Father hadn't come to hold you up.'

"Another morning he looked up and said, 'There's Father! Father, will you mend my wheelbarrow?' Then he turned to me and said, 'Father nodded yes.' He had never heard his father speak, as illness had reduced [the father's] voice to a rarely used whisper, so the 'nod' was evidential.

"Once Michael brought me a wet nail. In a puzzled way he

said, 'I stuck it in the vegetable marrow, and I heard "Take it out."' These three words exactly reproduced his father's whisper.

"The carpenter and an old Spaniard who sometimes came and worked for us both told me they heard Michael talk to someone while [he was] playing nearby, and that he had said his father was there. I questioned them and found that both men had told the child it couldn't be his father, as he was dead. The kind carpenter made a windmill for Michael and fixed it on the roof of a small house where the wind caught it and made it revolve. The child was delighted with it and very often watched it. One day he came running to me in great excitement and called me to come and look. 'Father's on the roof, and he's looking at my windmill, and *do you know?* . . . the wheel is going right froo Father!'

"We got evidence through Rammy, his Yorkshire terrier, too. One evening, sitting by the fire after tea, Michael was playing with his bricks; his godmother and I were reading. Suddenly Rammy stood up and 'pointed' fixedly at something we could not see, and wagged his tail. The godmother said, 'Whatever is the matter with Rammy?' and Michael glanced up from his bricks and said, 'He sees Father. Father's laughing at him. Hello, Father!'

"Some days later a friend we seldom saw came and brought her black Labrador with her. We were sitting on the big square verandah chatting when Rammy saw my husband again and reacted as before. The visiting dog got very restless, and whined and gave little upward jumps and barks. His mistress said she had never known him to behave like that and got up to go. When she had gone Michael said, 'That dog saw Father too! Wasn't it funny?' And then, 'Father did this . . .' (and he tried to snap his fingers as one would to make a dog jump up at them).

102

"When he was five or six years old [Michael] was patrolling the path in an English graveyard with his grandfather while his grandmother and I were tending their daughter's grave. He saw a black marble tomb with gold letters on it, quite different from all the rest, and he said: 'Granddad, what's under that?' His grandfather said brusquely: 'Oh, So-and-so [naming the person] is under that.'

"Michael: 'Oh no he's not.'

"Grandfather: 'Oh yes he is. He's dead and buried.'

"Michael: 'It's only his body that gets buried.'

"Grandfather: 'Well, isn't *he* his body?'

"Michael: 'He'll have an airbody now.'

"Grandfather: 'What's an airbody like?'

"Michael: 'Well, while I'm alive you can hear me coming down this path . . . fump, fump [stamping. Then, very quietly] but when I'm dead you won't hear me coming. I'll have an airbody.'

"I had never heard the word 'airbody,'" his mother said. "Michael must have coined it himself."

Michael's was not the only case I encountered in which a child described what he perceived as a finer but nonetheless real aspect of the human form. In this instance, however, the child was referring to his own out-of-body experiences (OOBEs), in which he seemed to leave his physical form and travel "in the air."

I talked to Matthew, then five, at his home in New Jersey. He seemed a completely normal child, intelligent and athletic, and though he was a bit diffident about being interviewed, his answers were forthright and matter-of-fact.

"Matthew," I said, "you've told your parents that you sometimes 'fly around' at night. Does this happen often?"

"Yeah."

"How does it happen?"

103

"I just wake up and ask God. Then I get my spirit body."

"Is your spirit body different from the body you have now?"

"Yeah. It looks just like air. I just go in the air and go where I want to go. A lot of times I don't go, because I don't want to."

"And what happens to the body you're in now? Do you leave it behind or do you take it with you?"

"I leave it behind."

"Is it night when you do this?"

"Well, it could be morning or night."

Matthew was three and one half when he began speaking of "flying" at night, his mother told me. "We knew about OOBEs," she said, "so we didn't discourage what others might have considered fantasy on Matthew's part. A girl friend of mine who lives across the street also knew about OOBEs. Matthew liked her very much and began to threaten her jokingly that he was going to 'come to her house' at night. Then one morning my friend came over and said to Matthew, 'You were at my house last night, weren't you?' He gave a silly grin and said, 'Yes, I was.' Then she said, 'O.K., tell me what I was doing.' He said, 'You were taking a bath and I flew around your finger!' She held up her left finger and asked, 'This one?' Matthew picked up her right index finger and said, 'No, silly, *this* one!'

"Later my friend told me she had been taking a bath the night before when she noticed that her cats, who were in the bathroom with her, seemed to be watching something moving about near the ceiling. She had never seen the cats act that way before. So she held up her right index finger and said, 'O.K., Matthew, if you're here then fly around my finger.' She clearly remembered holding up the right finger and said she had deliberately held up her left finger when she came to our house the next morning as a way of testing Matthew."

According to a survey taken at Duke University, OOBEs may be more common that one would imagine. Of 155 students who were asked, "Have you ever actually seen your physical body from a viewpoint completely outside that body?" thirty per cent answered "yes." From this and other studies a researcher concluded that "At least twenty per cent of college level young people believe they have had experiences of this sort. Of those who report a projection of viewpoint, at least seventy per cent remember more than one such experience."

Certainly the literature of parapsychology abounds with out-of-body cases. They are popular studies because there is often evidence, as in the anecdote of Matthew's neighbor, which can be substantiated by a second party. A woman in New York State, for example, recalls that at age twelve she was left at home in the care of a neighbor while the rest of her family made an overnight trip to attend the funeral of the girl's aunt. That night, the summer heat made it difficult for her to get to sleep, and she lay for some time half asleep and half awake. Suddenly, she seemed to be rising toward the ceiling, then passed through the ceiling and out into the night. It occurred to her at that moment that she might be dying.

She seemed to be moving toward a light in the distance. Once there, she found herself in a room where she recognized a number of her family, including her parents, and she saw in a casket near a window the body of her aunt. Though she wanted to stay in the room, some force drew her away and propelled her back to her own bedroom.

When the parents returned, the girl told them of her experience and described the details of what she had seen in that distant room, the position of the casket, the color of the aunt's dress, etc. They confirmed that she had described the scene exactly.

Another woman, living in Idaho, reported that during an operation when she was eight years old she seemed to awaken and see the surgeon and attendants bending over her. Then she floated gently upward and looked down on the scene, which included her own physical form lying directly below on the table. "None of this seemed unnatural to me," she recalled. "I watched the doctor and nurses for a while and then I had the feeling it was time to go back into my body." When she awoke, she astonished the surgeon with an accurate account of what had happened while she had supposedly been in coma.

In the course of my visit with Matthew to discuss his out-of-body experiences, one of his parents mentioned that at about the age their son's OOBEs started, he began to talk about "bunks" and "little people" who, he said, sometimes came to visit him. Though no one else had seen them, his mother told me, she hesitated to call them imaginary playmates. "Matthew has been extremely interested in them. There are times when he tells me they are there, or I hear him talking to them in another room, or he goes to the door and lets them in because he expects them." His father added that Matthew seemed quite definite about when the "bunks" and "little people" were and were not around.

"Imaginary" playmates are among the most interesting, and are certainly the most numerous inhabitants of childhood's other worlds. "When I was a child," the noted psychic Eileen Garrett wrote, "far from being alone, I had my secret companions: two girls and a boy. The boy and one girl were younger than I, and the other girl somewhat older. I called them 'The Children.' They sought me; I did not have to go to them in any particular place, or make any adjustments within myself in order to see them, be with them, or communicate with them freely. I saw them first when I was about four years old. I was in the doorway of the house and they were in the garden. I stood staring at them. I do not know how long we may have appraised each other, as children do, but nothing definite passed between us at that first encounter. I wanted to go out and join them, but I was unaccustomed to mixing with other children, and I suppose I must have turned shyly away. But next day I saw them out-of-doors, and again we stood and examined one another intently. Nothing occurred between us other than that strange feeling by which children sense each other's qualities and find their basis of companionship.

" 'The Children' continued to appear, and I accepted them. We communicated freely, but without words. Sometimes they stayed for hours, sometimes only for a short time. Suddenly I would realize their presence, and as suddenly they would be gone. Everything that I cared for was subject to change—the animals grew up and grew old, the flowers died, the garden withered—but 'The Children' did not change. When the time came for me to go to boarding school, I was fearful I might lose them, but they promised me that they would visit there."

Eileen's aunt, with whom the orphaned child lived, ridiculed her niece's accounts of her playmates, particularly when Eileen admitted that she did not know their names or even where they came from. "Just try to touch one of these children," the aunt said. "You'll find there's nothing there to touch."

" 'The Children' laughed when I told them that my aunt did not believe they existed," Mrs. Garrett recalled. " 'We are wiser than she is,' they confided. It was easy for me to believe this, for I knew that they did exist and that my aunt was mistaken. However, I followed her suggestion and touched 'The Children.' They were soft and warm. Yet they were different. I saw all bodies surrounded by a nimbus of light, but 'The Children' were gauzelike. Light permeated their substance.

" 'The Children' taught me not to regard too seriously everything that grownups said, and, finding my elders so often lacking in sympathy for the things I knew to be true, I gathered courage to face the consequences of insisting that I was right.

" 'The Children' also taught me to watch changing expressions of anger, fear, and uncertainty in people's faces—to listen to their voices and catch the meanings of varying tones and

107

cadences. Together we watched my aunt and listened, and though she was still the power that controlled my immediate destiny, I gradually lost my awe of her. By the time I went to school I had come to know that human beings never quite speak the truth, saying always too little or too much, overemphasizing one point or omitting another.

"I was eager to go where 'The Children' went when they left me, but, regarding me with a kind of pitying intentness, they were emphatic that I could not accompany them. I never clearly understood where their native place might be, but just accepted the situation."

Just how real were Eileen Garrett's playmates? According to psychiatrist D. J. West, "Lonely children sometimes conjure up imaginary companions with whom they hold conversations and about whom they talk as if they were real. But the emphasis is in the qualification 'as if,' for these children probably do inwardly comprehend the nonreality of their hallucinatory playmates, however loath they may be to admit the fact on direct questioning by unsympathetic adults."

But what, then, are we to make of the following incident, reported by Olga Worrall? "During the summer months," she recalled, "occasionally traveling ministers going to Washington, D.C., stopped by at the New Life Clinic. About a year ago two such ministers with their wives and children attended the New Life Clinic service. I saw five children as I stood in the pulpit (I was preaching that Thursday). One little girl in particular attracted my attention. She appeared to be about seven or eight years old. She wore a huge bow in her hair—quite old-fashioned, I thought. After the service was over, the children ran out to play, and I saw this little girl playing with the other four children. The parents asked if I would have lunch with them and I suggested we could all go someplace to eat. They said, 'That won't be necessary. We have our trailer and we'll have sand-wiches.'

"So we all piled into the rear end of this little trailer truck, and four children joined us. I asked, 'Where is the fifth one?' They said, 'What do you mean, the fifth one?' I said, 'Why, the fifth child you had in church with you today.' The parents looked at me and said, 'Why, we each have just two children.' So I described the little girl; I said that she was playing right out there. One of the couple's daughters, seven years old, spoke up and said, 'Oh yes, that was Margaret.' They looked at her with unbelief, then she added, 'Margaret comes with us all the time. She's my best friend.' She knew this little girl and was in full agreement that I saw Margaret.

"Her mother asked, 'Where did Margaret go?' The child an-swered, 'When Margaret has to go away, she disappears.' Then they began to question the child: 'How long have you known Margaret?' And the child said, 'Oh, I've known her a long time. She always comes to me when I go to sleep at night.' I'll tell you I was shaken because, to me, Margaret was just as real as that little girl who sees Margaret and knows her as her best friend."

In addition to companions in human form, there appear to be other, somewhat more exotic beings variously called elementals, fairies, nature spirits, or "little people." Perhaps these are what five-year-old Matthew called "bunks."

As might be expected, many of the stores of these curious crea-tures originate in Great Britain and Ireland. Wrote Eileen Gar-rett, who grew up in Ireland's County Meath, "I well remem-ber the women and old men who spoke of having seen the little people dance in the moonlight, and of the money which these old ones left, in some cave or hollow, so that the fairies would take care of the herd. Others told me that the 'wee folk' were benev-olent, but it was really a risky thing to offend them." However, she never saw them. "I watched for them," she said, "until the

109

dew dried on the grass, and searched through the spring and summer twilight, never, alas, to find them. Still, when you have lived by the banks of the Boyne and wandered there in the long twilight, you cannot resist the conviction that you are not alone."

It is the British, however, who appear to have accumulated more documented evidence of the little people's existence. "When I was a small boy of four years old," wrote the Reverend S. Baring-Gould, "we were driving to Montpellier [in the south of France] on a hot summer day over the long, straight road that traverses a pebble-and-rubble-strewn plain, on which grows nothing save a few aromatic herbs. I was sitting on the box with my father when, to my great surprise, I saw legions of dwarfs about two feet high running along beside the horses; some sat laughing on the pole, some were scrambling up the harness to get on the backs of the horses. I remarked to my father what I saw, when he abruptly stopped the carriage and put me inside beside my mother, where, the conveyance being closed, I was out of the sun. The effect was that, little by little, the host of imps diminished in number till they disappeared altogether."

To those who might dismiss Baring-Gould's experience as an effect of the hot sun, he offers another account from his family: "When my wife was fifteen, she was walking down a lane in Yorkshire, between great hedges, when she saw seated in one of the privet hedges a little green man, perfectly well made, who looked at her with his beady black eyes. He was about a foot or fifteen inches high. She was so frightened she ran home." And another: "One day a son of mine was sent into the garden to pick pea-pods for the cook to shell for dinner. Presently he rushed into the house as white as chalk to say that while he was thus engaged, and standing between the rows of peas, he saw a little man wearing a red cap, a green jacket, and brown knee-breeches, whose face was old and wan, and who had a gray beard and eyes as black and hard as sloes. He stared so intently at the boy that the latter took to his heels."

Though he never claimed to have seen the little people himself, Sir Arthur Conan Doyle, the creator of Sherlock Holmes, firmly believed that they existed and wrote at some length about them. "Children claim to see these creatures far more frequently than adults," Doyle said in 1922. "This may possibly come from greater sensitiveness of apprehension, or it may depend upon these little entities having less fear of molestation from the children." Each of Doyle's three children reported such sightings when they were quite young, and told their father "with detail, the exact circumstances and appearance" of the creatures. "Inquiry among friends," Doyle said, "shows that many children have had the same experience, but they close up at once when met by ridicule and incredulity."

America seems to have a population of little folk as well. "I can subscribe to fairy visions both from my analytic and my parapsychological experience," wrote Nandor Fodor, who practiced psychiatry in this country. "One of my patients, from Boise, Idaho, stated in all earnestness that she had seen fairies in her childhood. They were tiny people, running up her extended palm, dressed like human creatures. She took them for granted and used to tell them all she learned in school that day. Nothing could persuade her in later life that the experience was not real."

Francine Licciardello, an art teacher from Staten Island, told me that between ages two and four she had an "elfin" companion named Bubbus. He was about two feet tall, she remembers, and had the face of a man in his early sixties. He wore a soft gray cap which flopped to one side and a gray smock over tight gray britches. "My parents still recall my many references to this little person," Francine said, "and didn't try to deny his reality. I suppose they found this amusing."

A girl from St. Louis told me that she remembered watching

"fairies" and "elves" around her home—both in and outside the house—when she was little. "I guess they were about six inches tall," she said, "though some were larger and some smaller. The largest, I think, were about eight inches tall. They dressed in various ways. Some of them wore filmy things and others would have on very rough clothing, but nothing like what we wear. Some didn't wear anything. Outside, each plant seemed to have its own fairy, or whatever you want to call them. It was as if they somehow lived *in* the plants. Sometimes one would come out of a plant and mingle with the other beings. They would do this even when I was around. They never seemed bothered by my presence and were always very pleasant. Not pleasant to me in particular—they really didn't seem to notice me much—but they just had a pleasant outlook about everything.

"I don't remember when I stopped seeing them, though it was probably around adolescence. At that stage I wanted to be one of the gang. There was a lot of pressure then to be 'popular,' especially at school, which meant you couldn't be different. So I tried to suppress what psi I had. The result was that I stopped seeing the little people. I'm still aware of a kind of elemental light or presence around healthy, growing things, but I don't see specific beings."

The "little people" were still very much in evidence to a ten-year-old girl named Carla, who lives in Charlottesville, Virginia. From what she told me, they seemed to be a pixielike band that lived in and around her house. Among them, she said, was a character she called "Pied Piper," who played a long flute (though Carla said she couldn't hear it) which twisted around his body. Pied Piper was about fourteen inches high and wore a "short green thing" (Carla indicated a shirt with a serrated bottom) "and he has green tights and pointed-up shoes that twirl." His hair was "long" and "reddish" and he was usually found in her room. There was also what Carla called "an olden-day lady" who wore an old-fashioned dress and seemed to need glasses as "she's always bumping into things."

According to Carla, the little people went about their business without paying much attention to her, though they were friendly and "smile a lot." She talked to them, she said, "but not out loud, just in the mind." I asked if they seemed to receive these thought messages. "No," Carla replied, "they just do what they're doing. They do seem to talk to one another, but I don't know what they're saying. It's just a mumble of stuff. Maybe they're just talking faster than I can understand."

Carla regarded one of the little people as a "sly type." His pointed ears, slanted eyes, and cloak made him somewhat different in appearance from the others. She said she usually enjoyed seeing most of the little people, but the sly one seemed to appear when something "bad" was going to happen. She recalled, for example, that he turned up the evening before a school day in which she was expected home early from school to baby-sit. The baby-sitting job evidently meant a great deal to Carla, because it was on her mind all the next day. But when the time came to go home, the school bus broke down and she was late. This, she explained, was what she meant by something bad happening after seeing the "sly" one—"Not that someone I know is going to die or something as bad as that."

Not all of Carla's little people were permanent fixtures, she told me. When the family moved, some of them stayed behind. And at her grandmother's house, she said, there was an entirely different group of them that "don't stay around me. They're not mine." She said she also saw many other groups, usually around stone walls, when the family went for walks in the country, "though I probably don't see half of them." The ones that she did consider "hers" were found mostly in her room, on the back porch, and in a tree in front of the house.

There are still other worlds, or at least other beings, which

113

sometimes manifest to children. "One evening when I was about five years old," a young New Jersey woman told me, "I was in our back yard with my mother, who was hanging wash on the line. It was warm and already dark. Suddenly I felt an impulse to look up at the sky, and when I did, I saw the figure of an elderly man in robes holding the body of the crucified Christ. I stared at it for a few seconds (though it might have been minutes) and, as I did so, felt an involvement with the figures and a great sense of peace. I asked my mother to look up, but she said she saw nothing. After the figures disappeared I tried to describe what I had seen, but she simply ignored me and said that it was my imagination. No one can convince me, even now, that it was my imagination."

Marion Blaney of San Antonio, Texas, told me that "many times during early childhood I saw white-robed 'beings' who were surrounded by light. Usually several appeared simultaneously, and always at unexpected moments. My reaction was always one of tremendous joy. There was always telepathic conversation between us, but I can remember none of it now, except that I was told that I must not speak of these visits to anyone, including my parents. I obeyed them in this.

"The last visit was around age seven. I looked up one day and saw one of them, but the apparition seemed weak. I knew intuitively that this was the last visit because I was becoming too old to see them. There was some telepathic exchange. I asked if I could now tell my mother about these visions. The answer was 'yes.' Then he faded (all the visitors had always appeared to me to be male) and I felt terribly lonely. The sense of loss was quite profound."

What seems unusual about these experiences, in addition to their visual content, is the feeling of peace and joy experienced by the percipients, the sense that these were not simply external phenomena, but communications involving their innermost nature. The same is true of a number of extensively documented events which have taken place in Europe since the mid-nineteenth century.

On September 19, 1846, Maximin Giraud, eleven, and Melanie Mathieu, fifteen, were tending cattle on Mount La Salette in the French Alps, when they saw in the distance a bright light beside a place where, many years before, there had been a spring. When they approached, they saw within the light a woman weeping. She had been sitting on a rock, but as the children neared she rose and glided toward them, her feet several inches above the ground.

The woman wore a long white dress, white cape, a gold-colored apron, and white shoes. Her cap was of the style worn by the peasant women of the district, but wreathed by roses and radiating light. Roses of various colors were at her feet.

The apparition continued to weep as she spoke. Melanie recalled that the tears "did not fall to the earth; they disappeared like sparks of fire." Her message was that the people of the area had made a mockery of their religion and that, as a result, there would be widespread famine. Then she admonished the children to say their prayers diligently morning and evening and to make the message known "to all my people." She spoke French at first, then changed to the local dialect with which the children were more familiar.

When she had finished, she accompanied the children a short distance with the same gliding movement, then rose a few feet into the air and slowly dematerialized. A glow remained for several minutes after the physical form disappeared. The next day, villagers traveled to the site of the apparition and discovered that the spring where the children had first seen the woman was flowing abundantly for the first time in many years. The water was subsequently found to have curative properties.

The famine did occur as the apparition had predicted, causing

115

close to one million deaths between 1854 and 1856. Predictions of further calamities were supposedly given by the apparition to Maximin and Melanie, who eventually communicated them to Pope Pius IX. But despite widespread speculation, the Roman Catholic Church has never divulged the "secrets of La Salette."

Slightly more than a decade later, in Lourdes, France, Bernadette Soubirous, fourteen, was gathering firewood one day when she heard a sound like rushing wind, yet none of the trees or shrubbery moved. She turned toward a grotto and saw there a golden cloud, from which emerged the figure of a girl who appeared to be about sixteen. The apparition wore white and carried a rosary. Beneath her feet were golden roses. Somewhat frightened, Bernadette began to say the rosary. The figure before her smiled reassuringly and followed the recitation by passing the beads of her own rosary between the thumb and forefinger of her right hand. When the recitation ended, the apparition disappeared.

These and subsequent events at Lourdes are well known. Bernadette returned to the grotto three days later and again saw the apparition, which was not visible to her companions. Four days after that, Bernadette again saw the glowing figure, which spoke to her for the first time, asking her to return to the grotto fifteen times. The girl complied. On one of the visits, the apparition instructed her, "Go drink at the fountain and wash yourself there," and gestured toward the back of the grotto. Seeing a moist spot in the earth, Bernadette began to dig with her hands. Her family and friends, dubious about her claims of an apparition only she could see, were sure she had left her senses when she drank the few drops of muddy water which appeared, smearing her face and hands in the process. In several days, however, a pool had formed which, like the spring at La Salette, was found to effect miraculous cures. Today, the spring produces some thirty thousand gallons of potable water per day. A medical commission established on the site has observed and documented a number of cures at Lourdes for which there is no scientific explanation. Bernadette, who joined the Sisters of Charity in Nevers, died in April 1879. Her body never decomposed and can be seen in a reliquary in the chapel of the convent at Nevers.

Apparitions similar to those at La Salette and Lourdes have since occurred with some regularity. On January 17, 1871, brothers aged ten and twelve saw in the night sky above their village of Pontmain, France, a triangle of stars inside which appeared a beautiful young woman. Though the boys' father and other villagers who came to watch could see the triangle, only two other children shared the boys' vision of the woman.

In 1917, perhaps the best known of the "Marian" apparitions took place near Fatima, Portugal, seen by three shepherd children aged nine, eight, and six. There was a strong anticlerical movement in Portugal at the time, and the children were subject to extreme pressure by local government officials, including imprisonment and threats of being boiled in oil, to admit that their claims about a radiant woman appearing to them were a hoax, or to at least divulge the secret message that the children said she had given them. But the three resisted and seem to have been vindicated on October 13, 1917, when, as the apparition had earlier promised, a "miracle" occurred before some seventy thousand witnesses. On that day, a persistent rain suddenly stopped, the clouds parted, and a disc resembling the sun appeared. As it did so, it spun violently, emitting multicolored rays that swept across the landscape and the onlookers. Three times the disc plunged earthward, then returned to its position overhead. After recovering their composure, the witnesses found that both the ground and their clothing, which had been soaked, were completely dry.

As the apparition had also predicted, two of the Fatima children died not long after the "miracle of the sun." The youngest,

Jacinta Marto, exhibited various kinds of psi before her death, including precognition, clairaudience, and clairvoyant diagnosis of several physical disorders. Like Bernadette Soubirous of Lourdes, her corpse did not decompose. Though covered with quicklime when it was first buried in 1920, Jacinta's body was found to be incorrupt when disinterred in 1935 and 1950.

Fifteen years after the last Fatima apparition, five children aged nine to fifteen witnessed thirty-three appearances of a radiant woman in the town of Beauraing, Belgium. During many of the apparitions the children would fall into an ecstatic state in which they proved impervious to needles stuck in them and flames held under their fingers. Almost simultaneous with these events, Mariette Beco, eleven, saw a woman in a long white dress and blue sash in the garden of her family's home in Banneux, Belgium. Though none in the family of ten were practicing Catholics, the girl identified the apparition as "the Blessed Virgin." There were seven more appearances during the next six weeks; on one occasion, the apparition led Mariette to a small spring and instructed her: "This spring is set aside for me." As at La Salette and Lourdes, the water has effected a number of miraculous cures.

All these apparitions were studied by the Catholic Church and eventually approved as worthy of veneration. Since 1931 some thirty to fifty apparitions of the radiant woman have been reported, but only those at Beauraing and Banneux have received approval.

Still under study by the Church is an extensive series of apparitions (some two thousand in number) which took place in northwest Spain between 1961 and 1965. The story of Conchita Gonzalez, related in the next chapter, is also the story of those remarkable events.

CHAPTER EIGHT
Conchita

It is 7:00 A.M., July 1, 1961. Miguel and Serafin Gonzalez are eating breakfast in a restaurant in Torrelavega, Spain. Their meal is a thick soup, which will fortify them for the day's work.

A friend enters the restaurant and walks quickly over to their table. He seems excited.

"Guess what! An angel has appeared to four girls in your village!"

The brothers barely manage to swallow before they begin laughing. What a preposterous idea! San Sebastian de Garabandal is an isolated and impoverished hamlet high in the Cantabrian Mountains of Northern Spain. It is so poor that Miguel, eighteen, and Serafin, twenty, have been obliged to move to distant Torrelavega to find work. What could possibly attract an angel to Garabandal? Whose children have been mischievous enough to invent such a tale?

119

"But it's true!" their friend insists. "A taxi driver just came from there and told me about it himself."

Just then a man walks into the restaurant.

"That's him! That's the driver. He'll tell you himself."

The brothers' friend waves the man over to the table.

"*Tell* them!"

"Tell them what?"

"These two have family in Garabandal. Tell them about the angel."

"Oh, that." The driver studies Miguel and Serafin for a moment. He heard the story from a reliable person, but a taxi driver hears many stories. He does not want to appear foolish to these two young men who are smiling quizzically at him. Finally he says, "Yes, the angel stops by Garabandal each day to have some soup!"

They have a good laugh, Miguel, Serafin, and the driver. But their earnest friend seems determined to believe. "Yes, it's certain, it's certain!" he insists.

That afternoon after work, the brothers go to their uncle's house in Torrelavega. There is much excitement inside.

"Have you heard about the angel appearing to four girls in Garabandal?" their cousin asks. "According to the newspaper, one of them is Conchita."

This time the two don't laugh. Their cousin hands them a newspaper article which says that four girls in San Sebastian de Garabandal have reported seeing apparitions of an angel for almost two weeks. With the article is a photo of the girls, whom Miguel and Serafin recognize immediately. One of them is their twelve-year-old sister Conchita.

Miguel suggests they leave for home right away.

"No, we're too tired," says Serafin. "We'll leave in the morning."

It is the next evening when the bus drops the brothers at

120

Cosio, some four miles from their destination. They must go the rest of the way on foot.

Normally, it would be difficult for a stranger to find the road up to Garabandal, which begins as a narrow passage between houses in Cosio. But tonight the route is clearly defined by two lines of people, one line heading up to the village and the other descending.

Miguel and Serafin reach home shortly after midnight. There are mobs of people in and around their house, and it is all they can do to get inside. Pushing through the crowd, Miguel turns to say something to Serafin, but realizes others will overhear and perhaps be offended. So he keeps his thought to himself: "How peacefully we used to live! Now look at this!"

"Peaceful" describes San Sebastian de Garabandal, both before and after the extraordinary events which took place there between 1961 and 1965. To this day it is more medieval than modern. Most of the three hundred villagers, who live without electricity or telephones in a huddle of some seventy old stone houses, farm the rocky soil predawn to late dusk. Predominant sounds are wind, cowbells, and the assorted noises of sheep, goats, and chickens.

And sometimes there are sounds of children playing, though they generally keep as busy as their parents, performing household chores, tending herds, and going to school. But on Sunday, when the villagers do as little manual work as possible, the children have some time—after Mass and again after vespers—for fun.

It was in this quiet setting, on a Sunday evening twelve days before the return of Miguel and Serafin, that the strange and, to some, wonderful events at Garabandal began.

As usual, the young girls of the village were playing in the square. Among them was Conchita Gonzalez, the only daughter

121

of the widow Aniceta Gonzalez. She was a very pretty child, bright and vivacious, with brown hair arranged in long braids.

She was also a little mischievous. At one point, she turned to Mari Cruz, a younger girl playing near her.

"I'm hungry. Let's get some apples!"

Mari Cruz was eleven. She was almost as tall as Conchita but lacked her quick, confident manner. It would be something of an honor to go on an adventure with the older girl.

"Apples? Where?"

"Come on, I'll show you." Arm in arm, whispering like conspirators, the two hurried away from the square.

"Where are you going?" some girls called after them.

"Over there," Conchita called back, vaguely indicating a direction.

Nearing the schoolmaster's property, the two broke into a run, then stopped beside one of his apple trees and began picking.

"Conchita, you're taking apples!"

It was Jacinta, approaching with Ginia and Loli. Conchita tried to hide, and Mari Cruz started to run away.

"Don't run, Mari Cruz," Loli called after her. "We saw you and we'll tell!"

Conchita came out of hiding. "Keep quiet!" she scolded. "The schoolmaster's wife will hear you and she'll tell my mother!" She was the same age as the other girls, but exerted a natural leadership over them. In fact, within a few minutes she had recruited them into her apple-stealing scheme.

But before they began, Ginia was called away by her mother. Now four girls stood under the apple tree, plucking the fruit and stuffing their pockets.

"Concesa!" It was the voice of the schoolmaster. "Concesa, go to the garden. The sheep are roving around the apple trees!"

Stifling their giggles, the girls ran off to eat the apples where they wouldn't be seen. They stopped at a rocky path called the *calleja,* which led farther up the mountain toward a stand of nine towering pines.

As they began to eat, they heard a loud noise which they assumed was thunder.

The four girls did not make a likely band of thieves. Though occasionally impish and independent, Conchita was obedient to her elders and to the teachings of the Church. Since age five, in fact, she had wanted to become a nun. Jacinta, whose family was among the poorest in the village, was as retiring as Mari Cruz, though people found her charming and were often moved by the simplicity and sincerity she seemed to bring to her religious devotions. And if anyone represented respectability and the "establishment," such as it was in Garabandal, it was Loli. She was the second of the six children of Ceferino Mazon, Mayor of Garabandal and proprietor of its only cafe.

Not surprisingly, the girls began to feel some remorse for having stolen the apples. Conchita sighed. "What a shame! Now that we've eaten apples that don't belong to us, the devil will be happy and our poor guardian angel will be sad." She picked up some pebbles and began to throw them to her left, which, by tradition, was where the devil lurked. The other girls did the same. Then, wearying of this, they began to play a game with the pebbles. It was now close to 8:30 P.M.

Suddenly, Conchita began to act strangely, clasping her hands and making short, sharp exclamations: "Ay! Ay! Oh! Oh!"

The others wondered if she were having a fit. But she did not seem to be in pain. In fact, she seemed happy, almost joyous. Still, they were alarmed and decided to run to tell Conchita's mother.

But before they could move, they, too, were behaving like Conchita, clasping their hands and crying out in excitement.

Before them, they said later, was a brilliant light, in the midst of which, as if made of this light, was the figure of a boy. He seemed younger than the girls, perhaps nine, but had about him an air of great authority. He had dark hair and eyes and his complexion, too, was dark. His face seemed to them neither long nor round but was beautiful, and his hands were quite delicate. He was wearing a long, flowing blue robe. And he had lovely long, pale rose wings.

"Ay! Oh! The angel!" the four girls cried.

Suddenly the angel was gone and the girls were their normal selves again. Now terrified, they ran toward the church.

Their friend Pili saw them coming and was shocked by their appearance. "You look so *scared,* so *pale!* What happened?"

"We took some apples."

"And *that* made you like this?"

"No," one of the four said, almost sobbing. "It's because we saw an angel!"

Now Pili turned pale. "Is that *true?*"

"Yes, yes!"

The four continued to the church while Pili ran to spread the news. At the door of the church, the girls hesitated. Too full of emotion, they decided not to go in. Instead, they went around to the back and began to cry.

Presently, when they had composed themselves a little, they walked to the front of the church and prepared to enter. Just then, a woman rushed up to them. It was Doña Serafina Gomez, the schoolmistress.

"My dear children, is it true you have seen an angel?"

"Yes, señora."

Doña Serafina seemed very serious. She looked from one to the next, seeking some sign of deceit. "This could be your imaginations, you know."

"No, señora, we really saw him."

The schoolmistress knew the girls well and was fond of them. It would not be like them to concoct such a story as this. For one thing, they were not frequently seen playing together; they were friends, in other words, but not as close as one would expect a group of pranksters to be. For another, like most of the children of the village, they were truthful almost to a fault.

"All right, then," said Doña Serafina, "let's go say a station in thanksgiving to Jesus."

The station was seven "Our Fathers," seven "Hail Marys," seven "Glory Bes," the "Creed," and an "Our Father" for the Pope. When they finished they left the church and headed for their homes.

Aniceta Gonzalez was unhappy. She had asked Conchita to be home while it was still daylight. It was now nine o'clock and quite dark.

"Didn't I tell you to be home before this?"

Conchita suddenly felt weary and dejected. She didn't even want to enter the kitchen, where her mother was waiting for her, but leaned on the rough wood doorpost.

"I've seen an angel."

"What! Not only do you come home late, Conchita, but you bring a big story!" Aniceta had raised three boys before Conchita. She was small and becoming plump, but what she lacked in muscle and stature she made up for in her strict, authoritarian manner. "But I did see an angel!" Conchita knew there was no point arguing. She went about her chores in silence.

The next morning, everyone in Garabandal was talking about the girls' experience and had formed an opinion about what it really was: a big bird, a *real* little boy, a daydream, or even a bona fide angel.

The girls had forgotten their terrified reaction to the apparition and were happy to answer questions about it as they made their way to school. The derisive laughter of some villagers did not bother them.

Later in the day, Jacinta and Mari Cruz were intercepted by a nervous Don Valentin Marichalar, pastor of the village, who lived in Cosio. Word of the apparition had already traveled down the mountain. A conscientious man, the priest had made a special trip up to investigate.

"Now tell me, girls, is it true you saw an angel?"

"Yes, sir."

"How can you be sure? How can you be sure you did not make a mistake?"

The two smiled. "Don't worry. We saw an angel."

Don Valentin questioned them on the details of their experience. Then he sought out Conchita.

"Conchita, be honest. What did you see last night?"

Though visibly agitated, the priest listened carefully to Conchita's account. He was in a difficult spot. The Church had acknowledged the veracity of certain past apparitions, notably those at Lourdes, Fatima, and Beauraing, but its investigators had also turned up many cases that were judged to be frauds or hallucinations. A great deal depended on his own discernment. Moreover, what if the girls *had* seen an angel? The implications were almost more than the modest pastor of this rustic mountain parish wished to contemplate.

"Well, then," Don Valentin said when Conchita had finished. "If you see the angel tonight, ask him who he is and why he has come. We shall see what he says to you."

Conchita agreed to do this.

The priest was impressed that Conchita's story matched in every detail what Jacinta and Mari Cruz had told him. Next, he sought out Loli, who also gave him the same answers.

He now seemed more at ease. "Let's wait and see if the apparition comes to you again," he told the girls. "We'll find out what he has to say to you. Then I will go to the Bishop."

The girls agreed to go to the *calleja* that evening. But Conchita's family was against it. Aniceto, twenty-three, who lived at home, was sure the girls were deluded and that their families would become the laughingstock of the region.

"My God, what a mess you have got us in!" complained Aniceta.

"But there isn't any mess!" Conchita insisted.

When it was time to leave for the *calleja,* Loli, Jacinta, and Mari Cruz came to Conchita's house and called her.

Aniceta shrugged, perhaps influenced by the fact that the other girls had received permission. "Suppose it really is true and I stopped you from going." She sighed. "So go."

Elated, the girls set out for the *calleja.*

A few people along the way made fun of them. "Why don't you go to the church rather than that miserable rut?" they called after them. But the taunts did not bother the girls. Neither did the people waiting for them at the *calleja* who tried to shoo them away, nor the boys, hiding in nearby cornfields, who threw stones at them.

The four knelt and said the rosary. Presently the boys became bored and left.

Would the angel come now?

The girls finished the rosary and waited. A stiff, cold wind blew dark clouds across the sky.

It was getting late. Reluctantly, the girls got to their feet and started toward the church.

On their way, they met Doña Serafina.

"Are you coming from the *calleja?*"

"Yes, señora, but we didn't see anything."

They looked so sad the schoolmistress felt sorry for them. "Don't worry," she said. "Do you know why the angel didn't come? It is because it is so cloudy."

This did not cheer them much. They proceeded to the church and, after prayers, took their separate ways home.

Mercifully, no one teased Conchita when she got home. She

127

did her chores, had supper with her mother and Aniceto, and went to bed at a quarter to ten.

Conchita had just begun her prayers when she distinctly heard a voice. "Don't worry," it said. "You will see me again."

But the next day, Conchita did worry. The fact that the angel had not reappeared convinced most villagers that the girls had imagined things Sunday night. And her mother was adamant that she not go again to the *calleja*. "Why do you want to go *there?* Why do you not pray in church?" Aniceta said over and over.

The parents of the three others were also upset. They were inclined to believe their children—after all, why would they suddenly invent a story like this after being so truthful all their young lives?—but still, that evening, they worried as Loli, Jacinta, and Mari Cruz set out for Conchita's house.

When they arrived, Conchita and her mother were arguing just as they had the evening before. But now each seemed more obstinate.

"Why do you wish to make fools of yourselves? *Why?*"

"We are *not* going to make fools of ourselves. We're going to pray to see if the angel will come."

"No, Conchita, you can't go. The other girls may go, but you stay here!"

All four girls pleaded with Aniceta, but she was unmoved.

Then Loli, Jacinta, and Mari Cruz began to slowly walk away. They knew Conchita's mother was stern but not inflexible.

When they were out of Aniceta's sight, they hid behind a wall and waited.

"Loli, the three of you, come here!"

It had worked! They ran back to the house.

"Look, if you do what I ask, I'll let Conchita go."

"Yes, yes, what is it?"

"You three go now, alone, as if you were going off to play.

128

Don't say *anything* to *anyone*. Conchita will go by herself to the *calleja*, secretly, so no one will notice."

They obeyed. In a few minutes the four girls were kneeling in the rocky roadway, reciting the rosary. But like the night before, nothing had happened by the time they finished.

They began to get to their feet.

Suddenly there was a brilliant light, so overpowering the girls could not see one another. They began to scream. Then, just as quickly as it had appeared, the light vanished. Frightened, they stumbled down the *calleja* and ran to their homes.

Opinion in the village now became more positive. Though no one could explain what the brilliant light might have been, it seemed very unlikely the children would have thought it up.

Thus, Wednesday evening, Conchita had no problem getting permission to go to the *calleja*. In fact, at the girls' suggestion, a a number of people, including Conchita's aunt, went with them to the site, where they joined the girls in reciting the rosary.

But when the recitation was over and there was no apparition, the spectators began to laugh.

"Say a station!" someone suggested. The girls did this.

When they finished, the angel appeared.

He looked as he had when they first saw him Sunday evening, and they felt once again the intense bliss which seemed to unite the four of them with one another and with the small but powerful being they saw before them. They were oblivious of everything else.

Conchita asked the figure who he was and why he had come, but he only smiled, not answering. Then, after a period of time the girls could not measure but which seemed to them far too fleeting, the angel vanished.

They became aware of the people around them. Some seemed very excited and a few were crying. "When you see the angel again," one sobbed, "tell him to forgive us for not believing."

129

"If you don't believe in this, you don't believe in God," said another.

The witnesses said they had not seen the angel themselves, but from the look of joy on the four girls' faces, the fact that they seemed to see the same thing at the same moment and that they came out of their ecstasy simultaneously, it was obvious to all that something miraculous had happened. Back in the village, the spectators did not hesitate to tell others that they believed the apparitions were genuine.

Word traveled rapidly to other communities, and crowds grew steadily on succeeding nights.

They were not disappointed. On the following evening and for the three evenings after that, they saw the girls become ecstatic in the presence of something that was evidently quite real.

The crowds became so large that a *cuadro,* a square enclosure made of poles, was set up in the *calleja* to protect the girls. Only priests, doctors, and the girls' immediate families were permitted inside.

Some began to test the girls while they were in ecstasy. On Sunday the twenty-fifth, while the girls kneeled, watching the apparition, Conchita's family doctor lifted her about three feet off the ground and prepared to drop her.

Aniceto wanted to move to stop him but seemed to be held back by some interior force.

Then the doctor let go. Conchita's knees hit the jagged rocks of the *calleja* with a loud crunch that made the spectators shudder. When the apparition was over, they rushed over to her and lifted her skirt to inspect her knees.

"Why are you doing this?" Conchita cried. They told her what the doctor had done. "Well, I don't remember it," she said. "And it doesn't hurt."

The other girls had also been "tested." Their legs were

covered with marks from pinpricks, pinches, and fingernail clawing. Though disfiguring, these little wounds did not hurt them.

The crowds were disappointed when there were no apparitions on the twenty-sixth and twenty-seventh. This was also an embarrassment to a number of believers who had persuaded skeptical friends to come see for themselves. Some villagers decided that the apparitions were over. Others, mostly outsiders, took it as an indication that the girls were becoming afraid to perpetuate their hoax in front of so many people.

The day of the twenty-ninth, villagers noticed the girls' long faces and tried to comfort them with affection and suggestions. "Pray a lot for the angel to return!" the girls were told repeatedly.

That evening at the *calleja,* the onlookers seemed to pray the rosary with special fervor. Presently, the angel appeared to the girls and remained an hour, though the girls later said it seemed only a minute. They again asked him why he had come, but he did not answer. He only smiled.

At last, after another silent appearance on the thirtieth, the angel finally spoke to the girls on July 1. "Do you know why I have come?" he asked them. "It is to announce to you that tomorrow, Sunday, the Virgin Mary will appear to you as Our Lady of Mount Carmel."

The crowd was delighted at the news. Some sensed there might be parallels between what was happening here and the spectacular apparitions which had taken place thirty-five years before at Fatima, Portugal. People in and around Garabandal wondered if an experience similar to the famous "miracle of the sun" might be in store for them.

By the evening of Sunday, July 2, Garabandal was so full of visitors there was hardly room to walk in the narrow passages between houses. The girls had tried to go to Cosio that afternoon to meet Miguel and Serafin, coming from Torrelavega, but they turned back when many people walking up to Garabandal recognized them and plagued them with questions.

Around 6:00 P.M., the girls began to make their way to the *calleja,* with some help from several stout young men from the village.

Short of their destination, they fell into ecstasy and saw before them four radiant figures. On the left was the angel who had appeared to them before—the archangel Michael, they had come to believe. To the right was another angel who looked almost Michael's twin. Next to Michael was a glowing orb that Conchita later described as "a large eye which seemed to be the eye of God."

Between the angels was a beautiful young woman, perhaps eighteen years old, wearing a long, brilliant white dress under a flowing blue mantle. Around her head the girls saw a crown made of small, sparkling gold stars.

"Her hair is long, dark brown, and wavy, and parted in the middle," Conchita said later. "She has an oval-shaped face and her nose is very long and delicate. Her mouth is very pretty with rather full lips. The color of her face is dark, but lighter than that of the angel. Her voice is very lovely, a very unusual voice that I can't describe. There is no woman that resembles the Blessed Virgin in her voice or in anything."

The girls had no doubt that she *was* the Blessed Virgin, the mother of Jesus. Yet they felt no awe or fear in her presence, but an immediate affinity.

They talked to her of their own lives, of the work they did in the fields, of chores at home, of how their work outdoors had made them tan. The radiant young woman smiled and laughed in response to many things they told her. There were also serious moments, as when the Virgin taught the girls to recite the rosary slowly and meaningfully.

Presently the apparition said she must leave. The girls pleaded with her to stay longer, but she laughed and told them she would return Monday.

When she had gone and the girls were no longer in ecstasy, the crowd closed in and bombarded them with questions. Most believed that the girls had seen the Blessed Virgin, but others insisted that to listen to such "small talk" as some had heard coming from the girls, was beneath the dignity of the real Queen of Heaven.

One of those bothered by this was Aniceta. However, she was now much more inclined to believe. In succeeding days, there was more evidence to convince her. On the evening of the following day, for example, she became impatient for the girls to go to the *calleja*. "You should go say the rosary at the *cuadro*," she told them.

"But we haven't been called yet."

"What do you mean, you haven't been called?"

The girls explained that they were becoming aware of certain inner impressions that told them when an apparition was going to take place. "It is a feeling of joy," Conchita explained. "There are three of them—three of these 'calls.' The first is a weaker feeling of joy. The second is a little stronger. But the third one makes us very excited and happy. We only leave for the apparition site at the second call. If we left at the first, we would have to wait a long while at the *cuadro* because there is a long delay between the first and second call."

No one, priests included, had heard of such a thing in connection with apparitions. Some were quite skeptical. But they devised a way to test this: "After the girls receive a call," someone suggested to Don Valentin, "why don't you put two of the girls in Loli's house and the other two at Conchita's? Then, after the second call, we can see if they arrive at the *cuadro* at the same time."

Thus, after the girls reported a first call, they were separated and carefully watched. A half hour later, both pairs reported a second call and left for the *cuadro,* arriving at the same time.

That evening, the girls saw the Blessed Virgin, but there were no angels with her. When they asked her why the angels hadn't come, she smiled but did not reply.

In her arms was an infant, whom the girls immediately assumed was the baby Jesus. "He seems very tiny," Conchita said later, "like a newborn baby with a little small face. His complexion is like that of the Blessed Virgin. He has a tiny mouth, rather long hair and small hands, and a blue dress like a tunic." He smiled at the girls, but when they playfully tried to hand him pebbles from the ground, he did not take them.

This apparition lasted a half hour, from seven-thirty to eight. "Tomorrow you will see me again," the girls were told.

The girls did see the Virgin the next day. In fact, for a period of nineteen months, the Virgin and, less often, the angel appeared to them some two thousand times, often several times a day, though not always to all four at once.

Mari Cruz witnessed the fewest apparitions. As early as August 1961 she was heard to complain to the Virgin that she was sometimes excluded from the ecstasies. Then, in November 1962, she stopped seeing the apparitions entirely.

Between January and December 1963, there were no apparitions at all. When they resumed, with far less frequency than before, only Conchita saw them, though Loli experienced several clairaudient contacts with the Virgin.

Thus, Conchita emerged as the main "percipient," as had Lucia dos Santos at Fatima. She was the natural leader among the four, with a poise and quick intelligence rare in a girl her age from such a rural environment. And, though sensitive, Conchita seemed the best equipped of the four to deal with people's relentless and sometimes rude questions.

Many visitors seemed to have an insatiable appetite for evi-

134

dence that might convince them the apparitions were genuine. Fortunately, there was no lack of it.

While in ecstasy, for example, the girls often did things in unison when not in visual contact with each other. A film taken during one apparition shows the girls, their heads thrown far back as they stare straight up, crossing themselves repeatedly and performing other religious obeisances in complete synchronization, though it is evident that, if each girl could see her companion at all, it would be with only the haziest kind of peripheral vision. Even if they could see each other clearly, their movements were made with a rapidity and precision that could be achieved by normal means only after many hours of practice.

Further, the fact that the girls in their ecstatic states spent hours with their heads thrown far back was, to medical observers, a complete anomaly. To do this under normal conditions would, at best, soon cause dizziness and stiffness, and, at worst, strangulation. Yet the girls showed no ill effects from this strange posture.

With their heads craned back this way, the girls were able to walk rapidly forward and backward over extremely rough and rocky terrain, even in the dead of night, without stumbling. These extraordinary feats became known as ecstatic marches and were considered by some to be proof that the ecstasies, with their manifestations of greatly heightened physical co-ordination, were something quite different from hysterical states, which instead are attended by a *loss* of co-ordination.

As remarkable as the marches were the girls' ecstatic falls. Sometimes, while standing and gazing at the apparition, the girls would lean farther and farther back until, as if being slowly lowered by wires, they were finally prone on the ground. Presently, in the same graceful, dreamlike manner, they would rise up until they were standing again. At no time were these movements sudden or awkward.

135

Apparently, the "marches" and "falls" involved some form of levitation, a phenomenon not without precedent in the Catholic Church: St. Ignatius of Loyola, St. Teresa d'Avila, and Padre Pio, the Capuchin stigmatist who died in 1968, are among those who have been seen to levitate during moments of spiritual ecstasy. Witnesses at Garabandal found further evidence for levitation in the fact that, in ecstasy, the girls could often lift each other with considerable ease—they did this, they said, to kiss the Virgin— while two and even three strong men sometimes could not budge them.

On one occasion, the girls were seen walking four abreast toward a ditch spanned by a plank wide enough for only one. Yet all four crossed over at the same time, one using the plank, the three others walking on air. Another time, Conchita walked barefoot through mud (when in ecstasy, the children were impervious to the temperature or weather conditions), yet, when she kneeled to pray, her feet were perfectly clean and dry.

Another supernormal ability was associated with the quantities of religious objects—rosaries, crucifixes, prayer books—which were given to the girls to be kissed by the Virgin. These items were often piled onto a table in one or more of the girls' homes and carried with them at the receipt of the "call." After the children had held the items up to the Virgin to be kissed, they were invariably able to return them to their owners in the tightly packed crowds, unraveling with ease badly snarled chains and rosary beads, even opening the clasps of chains bearing religious medals and fastening them expertly about the owners' necks— all this while gazing in ecstasy at the apparition, never looking at the objects or the people in the crowd.

One much-discussed incident involved a compact which a woman left on a table in Conchita's house with other objects to be kissed by the apparition. Though some people were disturbed at the presence of this rather worldly item, the compact was the first thing that day which the Virgin asked to be presented to her. "Give me that. It belongs to my Son," she said to Conchita. It was later discovered that the compact had been used during the Spanish Civil War to smuggle consecrated hosts to condemned prisoners.

Someone close to the apparitions who was able to appraise their validity firsthand was Conchita's brother, Miguel. Despite his initial reaction that morning back in Torrelavega, he became a believer soon after he and Serafin returned to Garabandal.

Today, Miguel lives and works in Lindenhurst, New York. He is a serious young man who leads a quiet, somewhat ascetic life.

"I have never doubted the apparitions for a moment," he said recently. "I knew my sister Conchita well enough to detect easily if she were pretending or telling the truth.

"All the events so impressed me that I can recall them as if they happened just yesterday. The first time I witnessed the apparitions was the most profound night of my life. I felt very nervous, not only because I had never experienced such an event, but because I did not completely understand some of the things that were happening. For instance, during the ecstasy people were shining powerful lights into Conchita's eyes or sticking her with pins on her arms and around her eyes. In no case did she blink or give any kind of reaction to the testing. The doctors even tried to lift Conchita, but they were not able. Even the crying of the spectators surrounding the girls made me feel uneasy.

"From July 18 to October 1, 1961, I witnessed the girls in ecstasy every day. Sometimes there were one, two, or three visits of Our Lady between eight at night and five or six in the morning. After that year, I was in Garabandal only for Christmas and the summer, because I went to Leon to work as a mechanic.

"One time I decided to test the girls myself. There was much talk about how fast the girls ran when they received their 'calls' from Our Lady. I thought to myself, 'Well, they can't leave me behind. They are only twelve-year-old girls and I am a boy of eighteen.

"One evening in July 1961, at about eight, Jacinta, Mari Cruz, and Conchita were sitting in my mother's kitchen eating sandwiches. I don't remember if Mari Loli was there also. They had taken only a few bites when suddenly they ran out to answer their 'call.'

"I started after them, but before I reached the *cuadro,* they were already kneeling there. I had run as fast as I could but it had been impossible to keep up with them.

"The incident that gave me the greatest proof of authenticity of the apparitions happened in connection with a medal Conchita gave me. One evening she went into ecstasy in our house. She had many rosaries, chains, and scapulars in her hand. Although I was in the corner of the room, outside the circle of people surrounding Conchita, I could see her get up from her knees and give the religious objects to the Virgin to be kissed.

"Seeing this, I thought to myself, 'Why didn't I give her my chain so she could give my medal to Our Lady to be kissed?' I had no sooner finished thinking this when Conchita, still holding her hand up high and gazing up in ecstasy at the apparition, turned around, walked over to me, took off my medal and gave it to the Virgin to be kissed. Then she put it back around my neck."

Despite such support from their families and most other villagers, the girls were still troubled by the doubts of nonbelievers. A doctor in the city of Santander, for example, while questioning Conchita, threatened to have her committed to an insane asylum and her mother put in prison.

More typical were the endless questions put to them by visitors, most notably priests, who sought—unsuccessfully—to catch the children contradicting one another's stories, or committing some error in church doctrine. Particularly galling to some priests were the girls' accounts of receiving holy communion from Archangel Michael on days when there was no priest in the village.

One day a young priest was questioning Loli. "The angel cannot give you holy communion," he insisted. "Where would he get the hosts?"

She replied, "The angel told me he gets them from tabernacles on the earth. An angel cannot consecrate them, only a priest."

"Well, then, which is the greatest, the angel or the priest?"

"The priest has more power than the angel, for only the priest can say Mass."

"Well, if you think that a priest has more power than an angel, which do you prefer to see, the angel or me?"

Loli didn't hesitate. "Oh, the angel of course. He is much better looking than you!"

Even though they usually got the better of such exchanges, the girls grew weary of them and repeatedly asked the apparition for a "miracle" that would convince nonbelievers. Finally, on June 22, 1962, when Conchita was about to receive communion from the angel, he said to her, "I am going to perform a miracle—not I, but God, through my intercession and yours."

"What is it going to be?"

"When I give you holy communion, the sacred host will be visible on your tongue."

Conchita was startled. "You mean, when I receive communion, others can't see the host on my tongue?"

"No, the people around you cannot see it, but on the day of the miracle they *will* see it."

The girl thought a moment, then shrugged. "But that is only a *tiny* miracle!"

The angel laughed and departed.

Conchita saw the angel the next day and asked when the miracle would take place. "The Blessed Virgin will tell you that," he replied.

That evening, Conchita had an apparition of the Virgin and spoke to her of the promised miracle. "The angel said you would tell me when it will happen."

The Virgin replied, "On Friday the thirtieth you will hear a voice which will tell you." Conchita asked whose voice it would be but the Virgin did not answer.

On Friday the thirtieth of June, Conchita was standing near the tall pines above the village when, as promised, she heard a voice that told her the miracle—"the little miracle, as you call it"—would take place July 18.

On the eighteenth, the village was full of people, a familiar sight by now. However, not all were there for the "miracle." It was the feast day of San Sebastian, patron of the village, and some people were dancing while, elsewhere, others said the rosary. Some of the villagers, afraid that the celebrating would keep the miracle from happening, asked Conchita if she wanted the dancing stopped, but she said that the miracle would take place whether people danced or not.

Conchita received her first call around 10 P.M. and the second near midnight. This time she did not go out of her house, but, because it was late, waited upstairs in her bedroom.

At 2 A.M., the angel appeared to her. With her head thrown far back, she descended the steep stone steps from her room, went out into a lane by the house, then turned into a village street where she fell to her knees in a puddle of water.

Miguel fought to stay close to her. "I remember that day vividly," he says. "At about 10 P.M., my mother told me, 'Miguel, stand at the doorway so that no more people come into the house. There's no more room.' The door was opened so I sat in the doorway trying to stop the people from entering, but they just stepped around and over me.

140

"Then about eleven o'clock, I closed the door and said to Conchita, 'I'm going to bed because tonight there's nothing happening.' But she pleaded, 'Wait a little longer, because in a little while I'll be going out.' I think she had a call.

"In about an hour, Conchita went upstairs where there were some relatives and many other people. Later, she came down in ecstasy, went out the door and, in spite of the large crowd gathered outdoors, she was able to pass through. As for me, when I went out, I had to jump over people and squeeze through here and there. I had a very difficult time getting to Conchita. By the time I got there, she was already on her knees. I saw her make the sign of the cross and an act of contrition.

"I tell you this as if the event is engraved in my mind. She put out her tongue and in an instant—boom!—the host was there.

"I don't know where it came from, so suddenly the host was on her tongue. She kept it there for a minute or so and then she swallowed, made the sign of the cross, got up and left."

Another close observer was Alejandro Damiens of Barcelona. He saw a white disc about the size of a communion wafer suddenly appear on her tongue and remain there, he estimates, for two minutes. Damiens had a borrowed movie camera with him. Despite the poor light and his lack of technical facility with the camera, he managed to obtain several frames which show the white object on Conchita's tongue.

Also standing nearby was Benjamino Gomez, a farmer from Potez. "I was a little more than a hand's breadth away from Conchita at the moment she put out her tongue," he recalls. "I say it was quite bare, there was *absolutely nothing on it*. I could see her tongue quite plainly, and I assure you it didn't make the slightest motion. All at once I found the host before me. It was white, shining. It reminded me of the snow when it's iced over and the sun glances off it. But it didn't dazzle the eyes. It was about the size of a five *duro* coin [approximately the size of a

U.S. quarter], but thicker, as if there were two coins, one on top of the other. It was not quite round.

"Conchita's face wore that transfigured look this little girl always has in ecstasy. It was the face of an angel.

"Some people said she must have put the host there with her hand," continues Gomez, "or else, have had it in her mouth all the time. But I can testify that she didn't move her hands or raise them to her face either. Neither did she draw in her tongue before she stuck it out farther.

"Everybody who was there must have seen this, just as I did, and there were a lot of us. We all had time to contemplate the prodigy at our leisure and without hurry.

"I didn't believe until that day," the farmer concludes. "I say that because it's the truth and for no other reason. I'm not so Catholic as to let myself be taken in over this!"

Because the children seemed so concerned that people believe in the apparitions, some were surprised to hear Conchita say, in December 1965, "Believing in the apparitions is of no importance—if we heed the message."

But then they remembered several significant events.

When the angel first appeared, the girls had seen a sign beneath him but could make out only one word: "Hay"—"it is necessary that."

On July 4, 1961, the Virgin asked the girls if they understood what the sign meant.

"No, we don't," they replied together.

"It had a message that I am going to give you to announce publicly on the eighteenth of October," the Virgin said. "It is as follows: We must make many sacrifices, perform much penance, and visit the Blessed Sacrament frequently. But first we must lead good lives. If we do not, a chastisement will befall us. The cup is already filling up. If we do not change, a very great chastisement will come upon us."

142

On two June evenings in 1962, the girls glimpsed that chastisement. The first evening, Conchita was ill. After the customary calls, Loli and Jacinta headed for the pines, a large crowd following. But for a change, the girls stopped short of the grove and signaled the crowd to proceed no further. Then the two continued to the pines.

Presently the crowd heard, not the ecstatic young voices they were accustomed to, but a series of terrifying shrieks. The girls came back down the hill, flailing the air as if warding off something terrible.

The next night Conchita was with them. Again the crowd was told to stay at a distance and again there were the blood-chilling screams of the children, even more intense and horrifying than the night before. At one point, they could be heard crying out, "Let the little children die before this!"

A Franciscan present asked the crowd to pray. At once, the girls' cries and screams diminished. But as soon as the prayers stopped, the terrible sounds picked up, frightening the spectators to the marrow.

The event made such an impression that almost all of Garabandal went to confession and communion. To this day, residents speak uneasily of "the nights of the screams."

The girls will not reveal what they experienced, other than this from Conchita: "I can assure you that if it comes, it will be worse than being enveloped in fire, worse than having fire above and beneath you. I cannot say more because I do not have permission from the Blessed Virgin to do so.

"When I saw it, I felt a very great fear, even though I was looking at the Blessed Virgin."

But while chastisement threatened, there was also the promise of a glorious event which has not occurred as of this writing. In Conchita's words, it will be "much, much greater" than the "miracle of the sun" at Fatima. "The miracle of Fatima," Conchita

143

told a visitor, "is nothing compared to the one which will happen here."

"The Blessed Virgin advised me of a great miracle that God, our Lord, will perform through her intercession," Conchita announced on August 8, 1961. "Just as the chastisement will be very, very great in keeping with what we deserve, so, too, the miracle will be extremely great, in keeping with the needs of the world.

"The Blessed Virgin has told me the date of the miracle and what it will consist of. I am supposed to announce it to the people eight days in advance, so they will come.

"The sick who are present at the miracle will be cured and the sinners converted. There will be no doubt in the mind of anyone who sees this great miracle which God, our Lord, will perform."

Conchita later elaborated: "I am the only one to whom the Blessed Virgin spoke of the miracle. She forbade me to say what it will consist of. What I can reveal is that it will coincide with an event in the Church and with the feast of a saint, a martyr of the eucharist; that it will take place at eight-thirty on a Thursday evening and last about fifteen minutes; that it will be visible to all those who are in the village and surrounding mountains; that the sick who are present will be cured and the skeptics will believe.

"It will be the greatest miracle that Jesus has performed for the world. There won't be the slightest doubt that it comes from God and that it is for the good of mankind.

"A sign of the miracle, which it will be possible to film and televise, will remain forever at the pines."

Though Conchita may be the only one to whom the apparition *spoke* of the miracle, there was someone present the day it was announced who *experienced* it. He was a Jesuit priest named Luis Andreu.

The girls were in ecstasy on August 8, 1961, when Father

144

Andreu began staring upward and murmuring, "Miracle! Miracle!"

"We could see him," Conchita said later, "though in our ecstasies we never saw anyone except the Blessed Virgin. But we saw Father Luis. The Blessed Virgin told us that he was seeing her and the miracle, too."

Whatever Father Luis saw no one will know, presumably until the day of the great miracle; within hours after his ecstasy he was dead.

He was thirty-six and had been in robust health. Following the apparition that day, he rode down to Cosio in a jeep. There he met the parish priest, Don Valentin Marichalar. "Don Valentin," he said, "what the children say is true, but I ask you not to repeat what I have told you, for the Church can never be prudent enough in this kind of affair."

Then Father Luis left Cosio in the car of Don Rafael Fontaneda, heading for Torrelavega and Reinosa. He seemed elated. "You know," he said to Don Rafael and the others in the car, "I talked today with Father Royo Marin, the expert on mystical theology. He was there during the ecstasies. I can tell you he was as certain as I.

"I am so happy," the young priest kept repeating. "What a favor the Blessed Virgin has given me! How fortunate we are to have a mother like her in Heaven! There is no reason to fear the supernatural. This is the happiest day of my life!"

A little after 4 A.M., the group drove into the town of Reinosa. Father Andreu had dozed about an hour and awoke feeling refreshed. Again he exclaimed at how happy he was, at what a wonderful day it had been: "How fortunate we are to have a mother in Heaven! We must not fear the supernatural life! We must treat the Virgin as the four children do; they are an example to us! I cannot have the slightest doubt about their visions.

145

Why should the Virgin have chosen us? This is the happiest day of my life!"

He fell silent. Presently Don Rafael asked him a question to which there was no response.

"Father, what is going on?"

"Nothing. I feel drowsy." Lowering his head, Father Andreu emitted a slight gasp and died. There was a smile on his lips.

A clinic was nearby, but the nurse who opened the door determined immediately that the young priest was dead. A doctor quickly confirmed this.

"Despite the extraordinary shock of his death," Don Rafael recalls, "the others of us in the car had an indescribable feeling of peace and serenity. To the many people who asked us the cause of Father's death, we could only say, 'He died of joy!' "

A week later, while in ecstasy, the girls were told by the apparition that Father Luis would talk with them. The next day, she again appeared to the four and said, "Father Luis will come now and speak with you."

The girls did not see him but heard his voice. "It was exactly like the one he had on earth," Conchita said. "After he had spoken for a while, giving us advice, he told us certain things for his brother, Father Ramon Andreu. Then he taught us some words in French, German, and English and also taught us to pray in Greek."

When the apparition ended, the girls repeated to Father Ramon what his late brother had instructed them to tell him. The priest was astounded. The girls had given him details of the death of Father Luis and of his funeral in distant Oña in the province of Burgos. They gave a number of details about the special rites that were used, including the several exceptions to the traditional rules for the burial of a priest. Father Ramon could conceive of no way the girls might have learned these obscure details by ordinary means. As for the foreign languages Father

Ramon had heard the girls speak, they were all known to Father Luis, but the girls had never studied them.

In August 1964, there was another startling development concerning Father Luis Andreu. In a letter to Father Ramon, Conchita wrote, "Last July 18 I was told that on the day after the great miracle your brother will be removed from his grave and his body will be found intact."

If this is found to be so, it will not be unique to the Marian apparitions. As mentioned before, the body of Bernadette Soubirous of Lourdes, who died in 1879, has never decomposed, nor has the body of Jacinta Marto, one of the three children of Fatima.

"As he lay on his bed at the Reinosa clinic," Father Luis's mother remembers, "my son appeared to be merely sleeping. I shuddered, wondering if he hadn't been put into his coffin alive."

On January 1, 1965, Conchita was told during an apparition that, just as the chastisement of the world would be preceded by a great miracle at Garabandal, so would there be a "warning" before the miracle. "I cannot say what it will be, since the Blessed Virgin did not command that I reveal it," Conchita wrote to a friend. "Also, she did not tell me when it would happen. But I know that it will be visible all over the world."

In another letter Conchita said, "The warning, like the chastisement, is a very fearful thing for the good as well as for the wicked. It will draw the good closer to God and it will warn the wicked that the end of time is coming and that these are the last warnings. No one can stop it from happening. It is certain, although I know nothing concerning the date."

Again, in a report, Conchita wrote, "Jesus is not going to send the chastisement to discourage us, but to help us and to reprimand us for not heeding him. He will send the warning to purify us so that we may better appreciate the miracle by which he clearly proves his love for us and hence his desire that we fulfill the message.

147

"The warning will be seen and experienced everywhere and by everyone. It is like a chastisement. We shall see the consequences of the sins we have committed. I think that those who do not despair will experience great good from it for their sanctification."

Nothing more is known about the warning. Some people close to Conchita feel that it will happen a very short time before the great miracle.

The same day she learned of the warning, Conchita was told that the angel would appear to her on June 18 and give her a new message.

By June 18, four years had elapsed since the first appearance of the angel. Word of the apparitions had spread to many Western countries. That day, someone counted one hundred forty cars with foreign license plates crammed into the village. There were French, Germans, Portuguese, Italians, British, Poles, Canadians, and Americans. And from as far away as Taiwan came Father Marcelino Andreu, the other surviving Jesuit brother of Father Luis.

That morning, Conchita went to Mass with Joey Lomangino, a blind American who, at age sixteen, had lost his senses of sight and smell in a truck tire explosion. Joey's sense of smell had been miraculously restored several years before during a visit to Padre Pio. In March 1964, Conchita had been told by the apparition that Joey would receive his sight during the great miracle. After church, Conchita and Joey returned to her house, where they spent the rest of the day with family and friends.

At about 11:30 P.M. Conchita started for the *calleja*. She was escorted through the crowd by a phalanx of neighborhood men and federal police until she suddenly broke into a run, quickly outdistancing her escorts.

Somehow she made it to the *cuadro* and fell to her knees in the blinding lights of Spanish and Italian film crews. For the twenty minutes she remained in ecstasy, she stared unblinking in the direction of the lights. But as she emerged from the state, she had to shield her eyes with her hands.

For many spectators it had been a long wait to witness comparatively little phenomena. Many could not get close enough to see Conchita or to hear the loud "crunch" made at one point when she rose and then fell to her knees. And only a few heard the words she muttered to the apparition.

Nevertheless a feeling of joy permeated the crowd. Everywhere there were smiles and animated talk and strangers embraced each other.

Some of the excited talk concerned two objects seen overhead just before Conchita arrived at the *cuadro*. The stars that night were unusually bright. But something still brighter appeared from the northwest and circled overhead. Minutes later, a similar object appeared directly over Conchita's house, moved slowly toward the pines, then suddenly disappeared.

The next morning, Conchita seemed healthier and more beautiful than she had been for many months. At 1 P.M., a message in her handwriting was read to a large crowd which had waited outside her house.

"This is the message that the Holy Virgin has given to the world through the intercession of St. Michael: 'Because my message of October 18, 1961, has not been complied with and little has been done to make it known to the world, I tell you that this is the last one.

" 'Before, the cup was filling; now it is overflowing. Many cardinals, many bishops, and many priests are on the road to perdition and are taking many souls with them. Less and less importance is being given to the eucharist.

" 'By your efforts you should turn away from yourselves the wrath of God. If you ask him forgiveness with sincere hearts, he will pardon you. I, your mother, through the intercession of St.

149

Michael the archangel, ask you to amend your lives. You are now receiving the last warnings.

"'I love you very much and do not want your condemnation. Pray to us with sincerity and we will grant your requests.

"'You must sacrifice yourselves more. Meditate on the sacrifice made by Jesus.'"

In following months, there were occasional visitors to Garabandal, among them, in mid-July, a French pediatrician and his wife who had heard about the apparitions from hostile French newspaper accounts. The couple expected to find something of a tourist trap, with townspeople growing rich from snack bars, hostels, and souvenir stands. "We had an involuntary day of fasting," the doctor recalled. "All the townspeople could offer was bread, chocolate, and bananas, all of poor quality. We even had the impression that these poor, brave people were selling to us through kindness and not seeking a clientele. Certainly, we didn't see anywhere any article, souvenirs, photographs or pious objects of any nature for sale, even though we wandered about the town all day. No one tried to sell us anything. Everything seemed very ordinary, humble, and poverty-stricken.

"A priest we met on our journey to Garabandal had told me that one or two physicians appointed by the Bishop of Santander had called these children hysterical, victims of hallucinations and imagination caused by the great poverty and isolation of their out-of-the-way village.

"We pediatricians sometimes have to deal with young people whom we call 'pithiatiques,' those suffering from a morbid condition which is curable by suggestion. We are often able to detect cases quickly from their appearance and particularly their gaze.

"I can state my impression has been very much the contrary in the presence of Jacinta, Loli, and Conchita. It is rather that of simplicity. There was no affectation, and it still is a wonder to me that, after having been the center of attention and sought after, these children—especially Conchita, who was the most exposed to attention—behaved very modestly and did not try drawing attention to themselves or playing a role, even though they were aware of being the focus of attention and that people traveled thousands of miles to see them."

Another visitor was a social worker from America who came with twenty companions. When her group prayed at the pines, they were surprised to discover that the needles and bark smelled not of pine but of roses. And when Conchita kissed a small statue of the Pilgrim Virgin of Fatima which the American woman handed her, there was again the unmistakable smell of roses.

"As a social worker," the woman concluded, "I have been trained to pick out signs of abnormality in those I deal with. I must state that I was impressed with the normality of Conchita in every way. She seemed at ease with people, gracious, and most of the time, smiling. This in the face of requests from an endless stream of visitors to Garabandal.

"The morning we left, our cars began to pull out of the village at 5 A.M. The people of Garabandal, in whose houses many of us stayed, led us to the village plaza, carrying candles to light the way. They remained with us until we left, a truly gracious and charitable people."

At the end of September 1965, Jacinta and Loli left Garabandal to enter a convent school in Zaragoza. Conchita had hoped to enter a Carmelite convent in Pamplona. However, months before, Aniceta had requested an audience with the Pope. When no reply came from the Vatican, she determined that Conchita should remain in Garabandal until word came.

This was a difficult time for Conchita. Her two friends were gone, and Mari Cruz, still upset and confused by the fact that she had been the first of the four to no longer see the apparitions, had, on several well-publicized occasions, denied that she ever saw them at all. Doubts, too, had crept into the minds of many

151

villagers. "For me, when I see the girls in ecstasy, I believe," one woman said. "When it is over, I no longer believe."

To a lesser degree, this was also true of Conchita. When she had seen the Virgin as many as four times a day and received communion from the angel whenever the priest was not in town, there had been little time for doubts and little opportunity to slip into habits she felt to be wrong. In effect, she had been buoyed up, carried along, by the apparitions. But then, between late January and early December 1963, the Blessed Virgin did not appear at all, and after that she appeared only occasionally. There had been plenty of time for memories to fade and faith to diminish.

She was overjoyed, then, when in late October she received an inner impression that the Virgin would appear to her at the pines on November 13. This time she kept the news to herself but recorded the event in a diary she had been keeping since late 1962.

On the thirteenth, a solitary figure walked up the rocky *calleja*. "It was raining," Conchita wrote, "but I didn't mind.

"As I was walking up alone, I felt a great remorse for my faults and resolved to overcome them. In fact, I felt ashamed to present myself to the Mother of God.

"When I reached the pines, I began to take out the religious objects I brought with me in a parcel. As I did this, I heard the sweet voice of the Virgin.

" 'Conchita.'

" 'Yes, what do you wish?'

"Then I saw her. She had the Infant Jesus in her arms. She was dressed as usual and smiling.

"I said, 'I have brought you the rosary beads to kiss.'

" 'So I see,' she replied. Then she asked me to remove the chewing gum in my mouth. When I first saw her, I stopped

152

chewing and slipped the gum behind a tooth. But she knew it was there. I was ashamed and threw the gum on the ground.

"Then she said, 'Do you remember what I told you, that you would suffer very much on earth? Well, I am repeating it. Have confidence in us. Offer your suffering to our hearts for the sake of your brothers. We will help you and you will feel us near.'

"I said, 'Dear Mother, I am unworthy of all the graces I have received through you. And yet you come today and lighten the little cross I now carry.'

"'Conchita,' she said, 'I have not come for your sake alone. I have come for all my children so I may draw them closer to our hearts.' She paused. Then she asked me to give her the objects I had brought with me. I did this and she kissed them. 'Through the kiss I have bestowed on these objects, my Son will perform prodigies,' she said. 'Distribute them to others.' I said that I would.

"She then asked, 'Do you know, Conchita, why I did not come myself to give the message for the world? Because it grieved me to tell it to you myself. But it was given for your own good and, if you heed it, for the glory of God. We can count on you, Conchita, can we not?'

"I said to her, 'If I could see you always, I would say yes. But without this favor I am very bad.'

"'Do everything you can and we will help you,' she said."

Then came the words that Conchita had hoped she would never hear.

"'This is the last time you will see me here. But I will always be with you and with all my children.'

"'Oh, I am so happy when I see you! Why don't you take me to heaven with you now?'

"'When you present yourself before God, your hands must be filled with good works done for your brothers and for the glory of God. But now your hands are empty.'"

153

With that, the apparition ended. Conchita became aware of the rain once again.

She stood there a few moments more, a tiny, vulnerable figure next to the nine towering pines, then turned and headed down the rocky *calleja*.

"That is all," Conchita told her diary. "The happy times I spent with my heavenly *mama*, my best friend, and with the little Jesus are over. I have ceased seeing them, but I have not stopped feeling their presence."

CHAPTER NINE

Growing Up Psychic

*"Keep it to yourself, Joan, until you are
strong enough to bear being laughed at by fools."*

This advice, given many decades ago by H. G. Wells to the young Joan Grant, may seem a pessimistic note to be sounding on the threshold of what is being celebrated today as the Aquarian Age. Isn't interest in psi phenomena at an all-time high? Hasn't parapsychological research been given all the necessary academic and scientific credentials to be considered legitimate and even marginally respectable? Haven't "superpsychics" like Uri Geller shattered the monolith of public and scientific disbelief? All this may be true to some degree, but broad trends do not always focus down to specific circumstances. What is more, such movements usually suffer a backlash, which in the case of psi is evident in attacks by a few vocal scientific groups and religious sects (a curious alliance) on what they broadly condemn as "the occult." It is my strong feeling that, despite increased acceptance of psi phenomena, a young psychic today faces many of the difficulties which have existed in the past, and a few new ones as well.

Psychic abilities can bring certain rewards, to be sure. But it would be wrong to conclude this book with the idea that psi provides a ticket to a comfortable, carefree life. Too often, in fact, it has seemed more a curse than a blessing. A moving example of this is the story of a woman I will call Clara G. In response to the questionnaire I circulated requesting accounts of childhood experiences with psi, Clara dictated a lengthy tape. This was followed by an interview at her home. From the emotion present in both the tape and the interview it was clear that her early experiences were deeply felt and that she welcomed a chance to talk about them.

From birth Clara was an independent and somewhat precocious child. She sat up long before most infants are able to and played with the untamed mice in the house, who seemed to have no fear of her. At age two she had vivid dreams of great fiery cataclysms and of being spoken to by an awesome voice that, in her words, "came out of the air around me like nothing I've ever heard." She assumed that this voice belonged to God, the vengeful being her Christian fundamentalist elders spoke of so often, though it was hard for her to distinguish Him in her mind from that other unseen terror, the devil. Both, as represented to her by her family, seemed bent on punishing her, the devil if she was good and God if she was bad.

The conflict was complicated by the fact that, for as far as she could remember, she seemed to have her own inner sensing of right and wrong that was often at odds with her family's beliefs. As soon as she could walk, she danced with an abandon the others thought scandalous. At age four, she taught herself to play the banjo, which was also viewed as sinfully precocious. More offensive still, she once fashioned from reeds some "pipes of Pan" which she played gaily and expertly until they were snatched from her and crushed, amid cries that she was a "strumpet," a "pagan," and "the devil's child." As she told me, "I *knew* there was nothing wrong with any of these things and simply couldn't understand what all the fuss was about. I got into my share of *real* mischief, too, and could understand when I was punished for these things. But what I couldn't understand at the time was that I was considered strange, different, and that I was somehow to blame."

It did not help matters when Clara occasionally announced that someone in the family or neighborhood was about to die, and then, several days later, the person did die. In one instance, she stated that a young cousin named Mitch would die soon. At the time she said this, no one knew he was even sick. Mitch lived more than thirty miles away and Clara's immediate family was rarely in touch with him. "I said I wanted to go see him," Clara recalled. "When I was asked why, I said he was going to die. They said no, Mitch was not going to die, he was perfectly healthy. Only a couple of days later, my grandfather saw Mitch's father in town and was told that Mitch was very sick. Soon after we learned that Mitch died. When I went to the funeral, even the children kept away from me because they had heard that I'd known of the death ahead of time."

When she was eight, Clara awoke one morning remembering a strange but exciting dream. Her family often related their dreams first thing in the morning, in accord with a local belief that a good dream told before breakfast would come true. "My grandmother was fixing breakfast and the others were sitting at the table," Clara said. "I told my grandmother, 'I dreamed about *your* mamma last night. She's in heaven.' There was a pause and then someone asked me, 'What was she doing?' I said, 'She had a whole crowd of little children around her and a basket with her that was full of gingerbread and cookies, and in her apron pocket she carried peppermint candy. We were all sitting around eating gingerbread and cookies and later she gave us peppermint candy.' When I said that, my grandmother dropped the spatula she was using and said to my grandfather, 'Jim, make her hush.' But my grandfather asked me how Great-Grandmother was dressed, and I described her completely: a floor-length blue-checked dress and a matching sunbonnet and apron, except the pockets on the apron were larger than those on her dress. When I described that, a plate crashed to the floor. Again my grandmother said, 'Jim, make her hush.' Then, to me, she said, 'Pick up this plate. Take it outside and throw it away. You made me break it.'

"I did as she said. When I came back in, the grownups were in a very serious discussion, but stopped when they saw me. I was told never to talk about my dreams again. Only much later did I learn that this great-grandmother who died before I was born, and about whom I had heard next to nothing, had been described exactly in my dream. Not only was the dress accurate, but she loved children and used to carry a special basket with her when she went to town. It was always full of cookies and gingerbread which she gave to the children who always seemed to flock around her, and there was always peppermint in her pockets.

"Later I was shown the actual covered basket she used to use. I recognized it as the one in the dream. It had been made by the Indians and had two hidden catches that held down the lids. For some reason, I knew exactly where these catches were. I was the first person in my family to open it without first being shown how."

Clara is now in her forties and lives in a coastal town several hundred miles east of the North Carolina mountains where she grew up. Though the physical distance between her present and past is relatively short, many of the intervening years have been long and tortuous for her. She has suffered alcoholism and several times attempted suicide.

"I can't blame my family," Clara told me, a trace of North Carolina still in her speech. "They were God-fearing people—I mean really *afraid!*—and they thought they were doing the right thing by me. My mother told me when I was older that there was this belief that if a child could see into the hereafter, it wouldn't live. Naturally, they thought my premonitions about people's deaths, and especially the dream about Great-Grandma, were just that. So I can't be too hard on them. I just wish someone *knew* about these things, someone I could have talked to. Or even had a book to read about it.

"Now, thank God, I'm beginning to understand what it's about. I know I'm not a freak. In fact, I'm really beginning to appreciate my intuitions. I still have ESP experiences, but now I know other people have them too. Still, it would have saved me a *lot* of problems if I'd known that forty years sooner!"

Clara is by no means alone in the anguish she suffered because of her psi. "Relatives regarded me as strange and perhaps even crazy," said another woman who responded to my questionnaire. "Teachers are skeptical; a few were interested, although I felt they were silently laughing at me. Most of the kids regarded me as weird and perhaps feared me as well."

There were many similar comments:

"I was about thirteen. Everyone openly ridiculed me."

"When young I felt desperate and confused because no adult believed me."

"It hurt me deeply that my mother did not believe me. Now she admits that my psychic experiences scared her. She thought I was a strange child and couldn't understand me, and tried to discourage these experiences. She was also embarrassed by them

159

and told me not to talk to people about them because they would think I was crazy."

"I mentioned the experiences to my mother, but it was ignored as fantasy."

"My family, friends, and teachers thought I was strange, too introverted, and highly imaginative. I would say that up until five years ago the experiences upset and confused me. Now that I understand them, they are of help in many things."

"I am fourteen. My family and friends do not believe me at all."

"I used to pray to be 'normal.' "

Why all this resistance to psi? Why such unreasonable opposition to what, for countless people like those just quoted, is an ordinary human process? It is especially mystifying to me why professional counselors, psychologists, and psychiatrists do not take a more balanced view of psychic experience.

In attempting to explain this, parapsychologist J. G. Pratt has suggested that psi's great sin is to contradict a basic tenet of modern psychiatry, that man can and ultimately *will* be understood via known physical principles. "For many years," Pratt said, "we have been persistently calling attention to the fact that there are things people report, things that happen to them, which cannot be fitted into this concept of man as a purely physiological organism, however complex."

Another explanation, offered by Denver psychiatrist Jule Eisenbud, is that much of the phenomena associated with psychic perception too closely resemble, to the minds of conventional psychiatrists, the symptoms of certain mental disorders. "From the psychiatric point of view, there is every reason to be suspicious of a field of study which takes seriously a group of alleged phenomena and a set of propositions which correspond closely to delusions that have always characterized the mentally ill. Psychiatry has always taken pride in its discovery of the origin of these

160

delusions. They are regarded as residues of a phase of infancy through which everyone passes, a phase characterized by 'omnipotence of thought' and destined to be superseded by a less magic, less wishful type of thinking as the demands of 'reality' force the maturing individual to accept the world 'as it is.' One might as well expect jurists and officers of the law to find the values and rationales of the underworld reasonable and perhaps worthy of serving as the basis of a new system of ethics."

A third factor, with possibly more widespread effects, is what philosopher C. J. Ducasse has called "the will to disbelieve." In *Nature, Mind and Death* he wrote, "As a careful study of the history of psi phenomena shows, reports that a puzzling phenomenon was eventually accounted for in a natural manner, or that a medium was exposed as fraudulent, often have *themselves* been fraudulent or at least dictated by the will to disbelieve; for emotion is just as strongly engaged, if not more so, on the side of disbelief as on that of belief, and with a resulting equal lack of objectivity.

"Most people are highly disturbed by unexplained occurrences, especially if these relate to matters of practical import. Hence any assertion that the occurrence has been accounted for along familiar lines is easily accepted from eager desire for the intellectual comfort it brings." Unfortunately, one person's comfort can mean another's misery, especially in the case of children, who look to adults for an explanation of their perceptions and, above all, for reassurance, but receive instead irrational denials and punishment.

All this is not to say that there is not much to object to in the way psi phenomena are sometimes dealt with by their more ardent believers, those at the other extreme, and that an unusually intuitive child cannot be seriously harmed by an excess of parental enthusiasm. At approximately the same time Clara G. was experiencing her childhood trials in North Carolina, a child in

161

Pennsylvania I will call Felicity Harris came to the attention of an organization that was forming around the late psychic Edgar Cayce. According to records kept by the Cayce group, Felicity was intelligent, very pretty, and quite psychic. From the time she had begun to talk at six months of age, her mother told them, she had been making consistently accurate predictions. Mrs. Harris said she had written to several organizations involved in parapsychological research and had received a request to test Felicity from Dr. J. P. Rhine. But Mrs. Harris tended to view Rhine and his colleagues as "doubting Thomases." What she wanted for her daughter was a psychic reading of the type Cayce gave.

Cayce obliged with a discourse from an unconscious state which some of those present called "one of the most beautifully given" they had ever heard. In a past life, Cayce said, Felicity had been Elizabeth, the mother of John the Baptist, and in a subsequent incarnation was St. Cecilia. "Let each of you here so live the Christ-consciousness, as manifested in the Master," Cayce admonished those present, "that you may be counted worthy to be even as those who would gather the crumbs of wisdom that will be manifested through this entity [meaning Felicity]." Greatly inspired by these revelations, Mrs. Harris began to construct a shrine to Felicity in the back yard of their home. It was clear to Mrs. Harris that she and her daughter had important roles to play in the world. It was also clear that there would be a cross to bear: Mr. Harris, Felicity's father, thought the whole thing was nonsense.

Soon the local newspaper made a column available for Felicity's predictions. The child would dictate her prognostications to her mother, who would then prepare a draft for the newspaper, changing a word here and there to make the copy more readable. In time, however, it became apparent that more than a few words were being altered. The messages submitted to the newspaper became less and less coherent and took on a crankish political bias. When the newspaper challenged her, Mrs. Harris admitted that she had begun to write most of the columns herself. In fact, recent submissions had been made up entirely by Mrs. Harris.

The column was terminated and so was Felicity's reputation as a seer. In disgust, Mr. Harris left his wife, won custody of his daughter, and placed her in a convent school. Despite repeated attempts, the Cayce organization was never able to contact Felicity, though it received word in 1963 that she had married and was living, in her own words, a "normal existence." What she considered her "early unhappy life as a 'psychic'" had been abandoned when she was separated from her mother.

Just as the "will to disbelieve," described by Ducasse, can make many people blind to even the most clear-cut evidence for psi, there is an opposite pole of uncritical, unquestioning belief that can cause its own brand of mischief. Those who gravitate to the latter extreme tend to be blown and buffeted by every subjective impression which comes their way, or else rigidly and sometimes worshipfully adhere to some favorite source of psychic information. Thus it should be clear that those in close contact with children should be guarded about how much and what kind of approval they exhibit toward psi. If a child has unusual experiences or demonstrates a type of psychic ability, it is of course appropriate for the parents to offer the best explanation and guidance they can manage. But to the extent possible, this should be kept sufficiently simple and factual to enable the child to reach his own conclusions, if he chooses to make some conclusion at all.

One result of too much parental enthusiasm can be that the child assumes he will find elsewhere in his community the same avid interest in his psi that exists at home. A girl who, while hypnotized by her father, produced some impressive information about several of her supposed past lifetimes was led to believe by

163

her father that they were performing some great service for humanity. Perhaps she was, but only a few in her town thought so. The rest considered her a fraud, an egotist, an attention-getter, or simply crazy, and did not hesitate to express this. "I'd be a more secure person," she told me, "if at that susceptible age I had been allowed to develop securely along other lines, rather than having to handle the opposition I got." Even if a parent takes pains to warn a child against talking about his psi experiences to those who might react unfavorably, it is difficult for some children to be discreet about a matter which inspires such enthusiasm in the parents.

Too, a child may react unfavorably to his own psychic ability if one or both parents make too great a fuss about it. A psychiatrist reported that one patient, though quite psychic as a child, said she had turned against such matters because her mother was inordinately proud of her daughter's psi and of her own knack of making correct predictions. The child decided that if the mother displayed such unbecoming self-importance over what, to the girl, was a natural, God-given process, then she would avoid this herself by stifling her own psychic impressions. These impressions, however, resurfaced later in her life in the form of persistent and terrifying nightmares.

A third possible consequence of an overzealous approach to psi is that parents may subtly and unknowingly force their child into faking or exaggerating his perceptions or experiences. For example, if the child says he sees a luminous outline around a human figure, the parents may tell him with barely suppressed excitement that he is seeing auras. Encouraged by such a positive reaction, the child seeks further approval by attempting to see the colors that he has been led to believe are there. But as days go by, nothing more appears and he begins to fear he has failed. In desperation to keep his parents' attention and approval, he may lie and say he does see colors. After all, the chance of encountering someone with genuine auric vision who might be inclined to expose him are remote. Or he may actually begin to see colors. But this is no more a guarantee that this is an objective perception of the aura than was his viewing of the luminous outline, a common and quite normal optical phenomenon.

Though few parents are apt to go as far as the mother of Felicity Harris and build a shrine to their child in the back yard, there may yet be a subtler tendency to, in effect, erect "shrines" in the backs of their own minds. As some of the accounts in this book indicate, there is a potential relationship between psi and spiritual experience. But it is important to emphasize the word *potential*. Psi is a human faculty, not a virtue. It can and often does serve as a catalyst through which higher realities are experienced, but its presence alone is not an indication that the child who demonstrates an exceptional degree of psi is any more "special" than the one who doesn't. Parents who consider themselves well versed in the nature and metaphysical implications of psi should be especially cautious here. With their discovery and acceptance of such supposedly "esoteric" concepts as reincarnation often comes the prideful notion that being privy to such information and demonstrating a modicum of psi confirms their status as "old souls" who are more "advanced" and "evolved" than run-of-the-mill humanity. Unfortunately, there are any number of professed psychics, amateur and professional, willing to assist these flights of ego with a recitation, as flattering as it is fictitious, of a child's or parent's eminence in past lives.

Even if parents are not inclined toward such unrealistic attitudes, they should still be careful about how much attention they pay to their child's psychism. By the approval implicit in parental interest, the child may come to believe that he is expected to "perform" his psychic ability for them at regular intervals. The self-consciousness which can result may actually inhibit the free and natural function of the child's intuition, much as one's

165

breathing can become awkward when one becomes too conscious of it.

What, then, can be done to ease the process of "growing up psychic"? The following suggestions will not apply to all individuals and situations, of course, but they represent the best advice I have been able to collate from a variety of sources and from my own experience and observations.

Listen to the child who wants to talk about his psi experiences. For that matter, try within reason to listen to the child no matter what might need discussing. If it seems appropriate, reassure the child that others have had similar experiences. But try to keep such comments brief and matter-of-fact.

Keep a journal, if you wish, of psi incidents which occur in the family. Make entries as soon as possible after the event, since memory often serves poorly in these circumstances. Be sure to record misses as well as hits, such as premonitions which prove to be wide of the mark. If the journal fills no other purpose, it can be of interest and sometimes of practical value to a child in later life. For a variety of reasons, a child's interest in and ability to use psi often tapers off at adolescence. The journal may be catalytic in reviving this interest later.

Simple ESP games are an enjoyable activity that can be shared by both parents and children. These can range from guessing a series of coin flips or what hand an object is concealed in to working with Zener cards. If a Zener deck is not available, one can be made at home by dividing twenty-five index cards into five stacks and marking a symbol on one side of each of the stacks. The symbols used on Zener cards, for example, are a circle, a square, a star, a cross, and a wavy line. If you wish to "test" for telepathy, have the agent look at a card and try to transmit a mental image the symbol to the recipient. Guessing without an agent, that is, trying to determine the sequence of cards without anyone having looked at them, constitutes a "test" for clairvoyance. Five hits in a "run" of twenty-five cards is considered chance—that is, not evidential of ESP. In effect, the greater the deviation above or below five, the better the score. It is important to have someone other than the recipient thoroughly shuffle the cards before each run and make sure that there are no sensory cues, such as telltale marks or worn places on the cards.

Be responsive if the child indicates a particular liking for stories of the past. Several children I talked to who believed they had past-life memories made special mention of how much they had appreciated being read, and later reading themselves, a variety of illustrated histories of ancient Egypt, biblical times, the Middle Ages, etc. This should not be done with the parental intention of enhancing a child's memories or prompting him to talk about them, but simply to enrich the child's perceptions of himself and the world he lives in.

Be attentive to dreams which occur in the family. This is a particularly rich area to explore (though cautiously) and deserves special mention. Since much of psi appears to operate most fluently when there is a minimum of interference by the structured activity of the conscious mind, it is not surprising that many instances of telepathy, clairvoyance, precognition, and even past-life recall occur during sleep. Often messages which could not be readily comprehended or accepted by the conscious mind awake are communicated during the dream state. For example, a girl of twelve whose mother was very ill was sent out of the house one day to play. Presently she became tired and fell asleep. While asleep she dreamed that she saw her mother "walking down a beautiful avenue of trees, going away from me." In the dream, the daughter ran after her but soon realized that she would never be able to catch up. The mother then turned, put up her hand, and told her that her father needed her and that she must go back. When the girl awoke, she learned that her mother had died.

167

Evidently, the dream filled a psychological need for comfort and for a sense of purpose (helping her father) that would bear her through the difficult days ahead. In later years the symbolism of the avenue of trees appeared three more times in this person's dreams, at the death of a younger brother and sometime after that at the death of her husband and of a daughter's close friend.

Of course, most dreams are not as portentous, nor do they offer such clear messages. It is probably fair to say that, even if the contents of most dreams are remembered at all, they often seem too illogical and complicated to make any sense. Add to that the tendency of the conscious mind to distort and, if possible, ignore what is pressing up from the unconscious, and the prospect of making sense of dream messages seems dim indeed.

Frances Wickes described in *The Inner World of Childhood* a dream in which the symbolism illustrated a family problem in a simple yet vivid way. "Often with the death of the father or physical separation or a spiritual separation of a parent," she wrote, "the mother makes too great demands upon the emotional nature of the child and threatens its individual development. In one such case a mother lavished devotion and demonstrative affection upon the youngest child. She could not leave her even an hour or two without coming back three or four times to kiss her and assure her of her love. The child dreamed: 'I was out in the street in a big city and there were lots of bears and they were all chasing ladies, and a little bear came up to me and when he said his name was "Mama," I was so frightened that I woke right up.' The humor of the unconscious is illustrated in this dream, for the mother looks like a gentle and humorous little bear."

Evidently the child's unconscious mind found the bear symbolism the most effective way to convey a message that could be quickly understood by someone attempting to help the child, and, to a certain degree, by the child herself.

168

Symbols may also be a means by which the dreamer is encouraged to objectify some aspect of his personality, to see a trait or situation in a way that, by avoiding a literal description or illustration, prevents the possible interference of various emotions or conditioned reponses. Another case from Mrs. Wickes shows how an eight-year-old girl was given a clear but inoffensive picture of a personal problem. "I was walking with my mother," the girl said of her dream, "and I saw a little ball and I started to pick it up, and my mother didn't seem to think I could but I did and I started to pick it right up but it grew and grew and it popped out all over my hands and I got mad and dropped it and then it got small again and I went to pick it up and it got big and then I was mad and went away."

"This is an amazingly clear statement of her own problem in connection with any task," Mrs. Wickes said. "She flies at it without much thought or regard to advice; she is quite sure that she needs no explanation of any difficulty before beginning; she has tremendous self-confidence in her approach, but at the first difficulty is impatient. Then the task begins to look impossibly hard; she drops the ball, perhaps a little encouragement makes it seem small again; but another difficulty appears and she 'gets mad and walks away.' Her attitude is always that it is the fault of the task, not her own fault. That is to say, the ball has grown big, it has played an unfair trick. She does not look at her own responsibility in the matter. The child is a delightfully humorous and friendly little extroverted intuitive. She was quite capable, not only of understanding and enjoying the dream, but also of applying it. She had a sufficiently friendly relationship to make the little joke between us a cordial bond, not an impertinence on my part; so, when the dream had been explained and she had discussed it with a good deal of intelligent interest, it was possible thereafter when the quick, impatient discouragement appeared, to say, 'My, how that horrid ball is growing!' or if there were others about, to merely give a friendly smile and make a ball of my hands, whereupon there would be a little grin in response, and a new attack. I do not mean that this dream magically obviated the difficulties, but it did help in raising and facing the problem."

It is important to remember that what to Mrs. Wickes was "an amazingly clear statement," as she called this dream, might be a mystery to most people. She emphasized that nonprofessionals should be extremely careful in attempting to help a child interpret his dreams. "With the child," she said, "there is always the danger that premature interpretation will either put upon him burdens that are not his own, or else that even greater danger, that we will, in our clumsy efforts to understand the child, injure the mysterious process by which the dream is living itself out in his psyche and silently effecting its own power of transformation." Notice that Mrs. Wickes speaks of *premature* interpretation of children's dreams, having given her readers the benefit of the doubt that they are qualified to make even a *correct* interpretation.

Thus, do not try to coerce a child to discuss a dream. If the child volunteers the contents of a dream, listen and consider what (if anything) it might be saying in terms of the needs being expressed. A dream that is repeated or dream symbols which frequently recur often indicate that a situation is pressing for some form of resolution. Still, such symbols are a personal expression and, as Mrs. Wickes has pointed out, can, in the child, vary from those common to adult dreams.

In addition to giving cautious attention to dreams, try to be aware as well of what needs a child might be revealing if he appears to have an imaginary companion. If in Chapter Five I gave the impression that I believe most or all imaginary playmates to be actual denizens of some other world, or at least have some reality beyond the child's imagination, I should emphasize that probably all but a few such companions are purely imaginary. In both cases, however, the companion arises in responses to some need. Often there is the single desire for companionship, or perhaps for someone a notch lower on the "pecking order" to whom the child can pass along the blame or anger directed at him by parents or older siblings. But whatever its genesis, the companion is probably a constructive device and, in most cases, should not be regarded as a symptom that something is amiss. "The notion has got around that imaginary companions are evidence of 'insecurity,' 'withdrawal,' and a latent neurosis," psychiatrist Selma Frailberg wrote in *The Magic Years*. "The imaginary companion is supposed to be a poor substitute for real companions and it is felt that the unfortunate child who possesses them should be strongly encouraged to abandon them in favor of real friends. Now, of course, if a child of any age abandons the real world and cannot form human ties, if a child is unable to establish meaningful relationships with persons and prefers his imaginary people, we have some cause for concern. But we must not confuse the neurotic uses of imagination with the healthy, and the child who employs his imagination and the people of his imagination to solve his problems is a child who is working for his own mental health."

In the unlikely event that there are poltergeist phenomena in the household, it might be advisable to seek competent professional counseling to alleviate the literally explosive situation (see Chapter Three). A psychologist or psychiatrist with some background in parapsychology would be ideal. There are instances of well-intentioned adults asking clergymen to perform rites of exorcism at the scene of poltergeist happenings, in the hope of driving off the offending "demons." But it is important not to confuse possession-type phenomena, as elaborated in *The Exorcist*, with the psychokinetically generated activities of this "noisy ghost." Canon Pearce-Higgins, an Anglican clergyman who has

171

studied various psychic phenomena, has written that "there is not the slightest use trying to exorcise some 'spirit' when in fact wise counseling and tender loving care are needed." In fact, he believes that exorcism can be quite harmful. To most children, he says, there is nothing more authoritarian than the church. "If the church's authority is invoked [in the child's presence] in prayers or exorcisms, it only increases the pressure on the part of ourselves which often sets an impossibly high standard of behavior and against whose oppressive pressure the poltergeist demonstration clearly protests. It is as if an adolescent is unable or unwilling to run counter to such an authority consciously—by the front door, as it were—and therefore the protest comes out unconsciously by the back door."

There are other aids one could mention for the psychically gifted (or afflicted) child that would not differ essentially from what ideally might be provided for all children. Clear, vibrant colors throughout the home and in the child's clothing are preferable to dull, murky tones. Similarly, the music of such composers as Chopin, Beethoven, Strauss, and Debussy seems to create a far more harmonious and productive environment than the heavy, repetitious beat of hard rock, and especially the blare of radio and TV. (Several of the children I interviewed had stopped watching television of their own accord because of the bad effects they felt from it.) Creative outlets such as painting, dance, or playing a musical instrument seem to be especially sought by strongly intuitive children; ideally, there should be provision for these to be pursued both at home and at school.

The matter of taking the child to church is something that can be resolved only between parent and child. Some psychically sensitive children are instinctively drawn to organized worship, while others are repelled by it. A few may wish to go to church for a period of time, but then will enter a phase when they don't want to go near it. In any case, it is best for the parents to respect the child's wishes and not force him in either direction. Ultimately the best solution is for parents to be in touch with their own spiritual feelings and consistently try, as best they can, to act upon them. Then, when the child turns to them for guidance, there will be something honest and vital to offer them. "In spiritual education as in all other types," Frances Wickes wrote, "our first task is with ourselves. If we have no inner faith we have nothing to give. If we try to play safe and offer as true a thing in which we do not ourselves believe, the child gets, not faith, but insincerity. If, however, we have found our individual expression of truth to be still living, then in giving that we still give sincerity, provided we are willing to let the child, as he develops, find his own inner values."

Above all, parents should help children develop a sense of purpose, one that will give direction and meaning to their lives and thus to the use of whatever psychic abilities they have. Such purpose is not easy to impart, since ultimately it must grow from within the child and cannot be imposed by another individual. However, to parallel what Mrs. Wickes has said, if the parents themselves demonstrate a guiding purpose in their lives, the child will have an example to follow.

I, in turn, cannot suggest to parents an easy and infallible way to give their lives a direction worth emulating, assuming such is felt to be lacking. This is a struggle we must all make on our own, according to our individual resources and dispositions. I *can* say, though, that purpose should go beyond psi itself. From what I have observed, when being psychic or raising a psychic child becomes an individual's primary goal, a kind of aberration takes place. Egos swell and the spontaneity of psychic functioning is inhibited by self-consciousness and apprehension. Often the ability to produce psi actually declines. However, when it is but a

173

tool, a means, in the service of some meaningful and fulfilling end, or even in the dedicated search for such an end, then psi finds its best expression. Then "growing up psychic" does not mean the development of one aspect of an individual, but growth of the total being.

Index

specific cases, individuals, kinds)
Predictions (prophecies), 74–78,
162–63, 164 (*see also* Intuition;
Precognition; Premonitions;
specific cases, individuals,
kinds); accidents and disasters
and, 5–7 (*see also* Accidents);
and death, 74–76, 157, 159,
167–68; and recall of previous
lives, 87–88; and visions,
115–16, 117–18
Premonitions, 31, 73–78 (*see also*
Intuition; Precognition;
Predictions); of accidents and
disasters, 5–7 (*see also*
Accidents)
Prophecies. *See* Predictions
Psi (psi phenomena), viii, ix
(*see also* Extrasensory
perception; specific kinds);
forms of, ix, 2 (*see also* specific
kinds); increased interest in and
acceptance of, 155–56; potential
relationship between spiritual
experience and, 165; and
problems of "growing up
psychic," 155–67; resistance to,
155–61; use of term, viii n., ix
Psychiatry (psychiatrists), and psi
phenomena, 160–61
Psychic magazine, 97
Psychics, 165
"Psychoed, The" (Mearns), 99 n.
Psychokinesis (PK), 43–52 (*see
also* specific aspects, cases,
developments, effects,
individuals); healing and, 48,
53–72; poltergeist phenomena
and, 45–48, 171–72; power of,
43–52; use of term, viii n.
Psychometry, as an aspect of
clairvoyance, 13–14
Psychosomatic ailments and
disorders, healing and, 52, 69
Purpose (sense of direction),
psychically gifted children and,
173–74

Recollections (memories),

past-life, 78–84, 86–97, 167. *See
also* Reincarnation
Reincarnation, 78–84, 86–97, 101,
163–64, 165, 167 (*see also*
specific cases, individuals,
places); continuum of existence
and, 78–84, 86–87; hypnosis
and, 163–64
Religion, psi phenomena and, ix
(*see also* Church, the; Roman
Catholic Church; specific
aspects, cases, individuals,
places); and apparitions and
visions, 115–18, 136–42 (*see
also* Apparitions; Jesus; Marian
apparitions); healing and,
51, 53–72; past-life memories
and, 86, 89–90; psychically
gifted children and, 172–73
Religious objects, apparitions and
blessing of, 136–42
Repressions, poltergeist
phenomena and, 48
Rheumatism, healing of, 50
Rhine, Dr. J. P., 162
Rhine, Dr. Louisa, 75, 100
Rodriquez, Joaquina, 57–58
Roman Catholic Church, 116, 118,
126, 136

Samona, Alexandrina, 83–84
Sand, George, 78
San Sebastian de Garabandal,
Spain, 119–54
Schmeidler, Dr. Gertrude, 48
School situations, psi phenomena
in, 8–9. *See also* Classroom
situations; Exams
Schopenhauer, Arthur, 78–79
Schwarz, Ardis, 3
Schwarz, Dr. Berthold, 3–4
Schwarz, Eric, 3
Schwarz, Lisa, 3–4
Search in Secret India, A
(Brunton), 90
Senders (agents). *See* Agents and
percipients